NAIL IT …
with the "3 Skills"

The True Fundamentals
of Golf

By
JOE HAGAN PGA

Photography by:
Laurie Haskell

Illustrations by:
Shelley Fleming

Front Cover Photography by:
Mike Hall

Designed and Printed by:
Alphaset Digital Limited.
Telephone: 0871 222 2699
www.alphaset.co.uk

Acknowledgments:

David Esser, for your kindness and for making it all possible.

Terry Moore and everyone at Alphaset, for your professionalism, creativity, attention to detail and tireless hard work.

Laurie Haskell and Henry at Haskell Photography, Lancaster Mews, London. I cannot thank you both enough for your hard work and skilful photography.

Shelley Fleming, for your patience with me and interpreting my ideas so well in the illustrations, you're very special.

Kevin McDonald, for your belief, encouragement and support right from the start.

Marion Hoyland Chow, thank you so much and sorry for being such a pain!

Rodney Hutton, Dean, Mara and all the fantastic staff at Hersham Village Golf Club.

Mike Hall, your input was really important, thank you so much.

Steve and Celia Whitehead, Steve Harris and Ed Scott, big thank you's to all of you.

My family and close friends for always being there and encouraging me to write.

Finally thank you to anyone who has ever taken a golf lesson from me, you have all contributed to this book whether you know it or not.

Without the input from all the wonderful people mentioned above, this publication would never have been possible. The help and support you have given me has been overwhelming, I will always be indebted to you.

Contents

For Mum and Dad with all my love

Introduction

Like many before me, my first solid, powerful golf shot got me completely hooked on the game and created a lifelong fascination with this wonderful sport.

I have been teaching golf for more than 23 years and for the last 12 it has been my full time occupation. In that time my passion for teaching has grown stronger and stronger. For me, it's a bit like Christmas. When I was a kid, receiving presents was incredibly exciting, but as I got older it became a lot more pleasurable to give presents. That's how I feel about teaching. When I see someone improve and benefit from the coaching I have given it feels more pleasurable than playing the game well myself. To help a pupil improve at anything, let alone golf, can be wonderfully rewarding and leaves the teacher with a great sense of worth.

So for me it was always frustrating when in trying to help a pupil, I sometimes found that for all my effort, it would not always be successful. I remember attending a coaching conference many years ago and hearing a top coach say that, "achieving a 30% success rate with pupils was very good – in coaching terms". This statement left me flabbergasted, I was determined to be better than that! A 30% success rate to me was simply not good enough.

From then on, I immersed myself in golf tuition books, articles, DVDs and teaching gadgets. I attended coaching conferences in Europe, America and New Zealand to listen to the best coaches and their ideas and philosophies. I wanted to become an authority on the subject, knowing more than anyone else.

However, all that happened is that I became bogged down and frustrated by all the conflicting theories and techniques put forward. I also started to hear depressing statistics that claimed "average handicaps have not changed in some 40 years" and "80% of golfers never break a 100", despite the fact that manufacturers have made huge strides forward with equipment and golf ball technology.

It seemed to me that the only real improvements were being made at the top echelons of the professional game, whilst the average handicap player was being left totally behind. There *had* to be a reason for this lack of improvement.

I then began to explore this problem with my pupils themselves. I began asking *them* more questions about what they thought about their game and asking them what *they* believed needed to be done in order to achieve improvement. Listening to their answers, it slowly began to dawn on me why the aforementioned depressing statistics exist.

Whilst all these golfers had an abundance of theories on swing technique and how they should move their bodies in the process (varying from simple to highly complex), virtually all the golfers I questioned had no real idea whatsoever of the correct way to apply the club *itself* to the ball through impact.

And the reason why? BECAUSE NO ONE HAD EVER TOLD THEM! Simple as that!

Ultimately therefore, it wasn't until I started listening to my own pupils that I learnt a huge majority of golfers suffer from a total misconception of what actually happens at impact when a good shot is struck. I understood then that ball striking improvement for these players was not possible as long as these misconceptions existed in their minds.

I then began experimenting with my pupils by setting them very focused tasks to achieve at impact with the club head and to totally forget about their swing altogether. **The initial results amazed me**. Very quickly their ball striking quality improved beyond recognition, but what astonished me more was that their swings started to change for the better totally subconsciously. I was really onto something!

Swing changes that previously required a great deal of thought process and discomfort to the pupil I could now effect upon them without any paralysing swing thoughts whatsoever, as long as their correct perception of impact was applied. This seemed too good to be true!

Thinking more deeply on this subject led me to the following conclusion.

"The golf swing happens as a result of the players pre-determined use of the club through impact to effect the desired ball flight."

This statement explains to a large degree why players always seem to say after playing a great game that they didn't have to think of the swing at all, just the outcome of the shot.

This same statement also has a downside too, since if the pre-determined use of the club through impact is incorrectly perceived, the resultant swing can only be incorrect too – and this is exactly the predicament in which a vast majority of the world's golfers find themselves in - no wonder only 20% of them ever break a 100!

What this book will do for you is outline very clearly the tasks that you *have* to achieve with the club head at impact and how to practice them. I have broken down these tasks to just three things, so all you have to learn is 3 skills, **that's all it is, just 3 skills to master consistent good ball striking forever**.

Also, more good news is that these are very natural skills that everyone regardless of age, or physical ability can apply very easily with practice. They are most definitely not technically difficult skills and are best applied *without* any swing thoughts at all. When you apply these 3 skills with the club head to the ball you will be guaranteed a crisp, solid contact and you will see the ball fly powerfully and effortlessly in the right direction. The more you practice these skills, the better your ball striking will become.

The appeal of this book is universal, however the players who will gain most from it are the golfing majority ie. anybody playing above a low single figure handicap. For those golfers playing in low single figures or better, the chances are you will already be applying the 3 skills and that is why you are in that category already. Nevertheless, you will learn an awful lot from the simple effectiveness of this books' overall philosophy. It is a philosophy which will open up a pathway to further improvement even for the very best players.

Part One
observations and facts you must read.

"Everything should be made as simple as possible, but not simpler"
(Albert Einstein)

Chapter
One

"LET THE CLUB DO
THE WORK!"

DO YOU REALLY KNOW WHAT THIS MEANS?

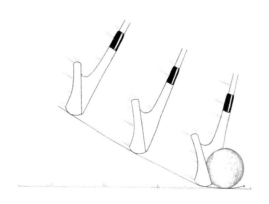

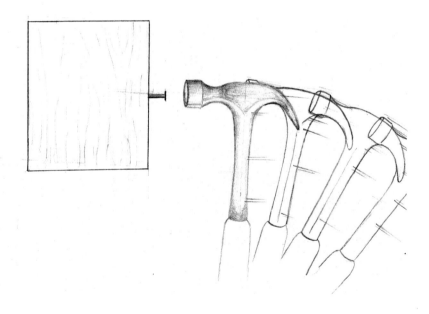

"Just let the club do the work!"

I think you'll agree that virtually every golfer has used this phrase or had it said to them at some time. I find it a very interesting statement.

Do a little test for me, get a few of your golfing friends together and ask them about this phrase. Without letting them communicate with each other, get them to individually write down how we "let the club do the work", when we hit a powerful, effortless golf shot.

How many wrote down something similar to this statement:-
"To let the club do the work we have to apply pressure to the ball as squarely as possible with the club's sweet spot."

At a guess I would say virtually no golfers answered it in this way. In my experience I have rarely heard anyone answer it along these lines.

Over complicating affairs

You will notice from your friends' answers that some will be highly complicated and long winded, most will talk about parts of their body and will have elaborate swing theories attached. *All* of the answers will vary a great deal from person to person and some will have trouble writing anything down at all because they will perceive that the answer is so difficult that they really would not know where to start.

Very few people will answer it in the simple, short and precise sentence mentioned, merely because their minds will not allow them to think that succinctly on a subject they see as being so highly complex.

I think this is a good reflection of how most players approach the game. They over complicate it totally unnecessarily and find it hard to think in the simple, clear-cut way that it should be.

Imagine if the question I had set instead was:
"Outline how we let a hammer do its job when we drive a nail into a block of wood."

Would the answers have generally stretched beyond:
"We have to hit the nail squarely on its head with enough force from the head of the hammer."

Probably not, but then you might say, the *task* in this exercise is so much clearer, so what we allow the hammer to do is much easier to describe, and you would be right!

Keeping the task in mind

The problem with golf is that the *task* is never identified as clearly as it should be and our *focus* is taken away from the only point that matters (impact) and drawn instead into a myriad of other irrelevant areas (usually our body or our swing).

When you consider the ball will only receive directions as to how it will fly from its collision with the club head, just as the nail only receives directions from the hammerhead, I would regard the loss of focus in this area as a seriously big oversight, wouldn't you agree?

Now, don't get me wrong, I'm not saying hitting a golf shot is as easy as driving a nail into wood. The former definitely requires the greater skill. However, I do believe the thought process behind applying the skill should be the same for either task, after all, a golf club is a tool for a job just like a hammer is too.

The typical golfer's mindset

Let me give you an example of a typical golfer's mindset.

If you ask a golfer who has hit an off-target shot with poor contact why that has happened, their answer will invariably be because "their right shoulder came over the top" or "their swing was off plane" or "their head came up too soon" or "their body got ahead of their arms" etc. etc., the list is endless. Virtually *never* will the golfer say "the clubface was not applied in the right way at impact", but that's what happened! The golf ball only reacts to the last statement, it does not care about any of the former remarks!

However, if you asked a person when they have made poor contact with a nail, what happened, their answer invariably would be "because I didn't hit the nail squarely with the hammer". Their answer would be no more complex than that and they certainly would not analyse what went wrong and try and correct it, they would just keep practicing with the task in mind until they got better at it.

All this begs the question . . .

"How did golfers allow their thinking to become so complicated?"

I believe it's because the skills of impact, the real task, are *never* outlined to us. Instead, from the very first day a golfer picks up a club they are force fed intricate swing theory and exposed to rules that they are led to believe they must stick to. Certainly every golf tuition book, magazine article, DVD and golf swing commentary on TV, support this overly complex approach, so it's not hard to understand that if anyone absorbs this material for long enough, they will become accustomed to this way of thinking as being the norm.

"It doesn't have to be that way"

One of my primary goals in this book is to convince you that thinking this way should most definitely *not* be the norm. That is why you will not hear any references from me whatsoever, to any form of swing theory or ways that you have to move your body. I *will* show you how good ball strikers use the golf club at impact though, and I *will* explain the three skills we can *all* master, those that the good ball strikers are using. These skills I will show you can be practiced individually then blended together seamlessly and you really will feel how "the club does the work!"

Actions, not thoughts!

Also, remember this, these three skills are *not* swing thoughts, they are *actions*, which when practiced enough, are executed without conscious thought. This then leaves the player free to focus on the intended outcome of the shot, a state of mind I think we all feel when playing at our best. It is similar to changing gear in a car. Initially this is quite a tricky skill to acquire, but soon with practice, we virtually all master it and it leaves us free to focus on driving the car to our destination instead.

Let us now examine in closer detail the 3 skills these good consistent ball strikers ALL use through impact and why they are so significant.

An apology to left handed golfers.

All references, illustrations and photos in this book are intended for right handed golfers. For the left handed golfing population I can understand this must be terribly frustrating and can only apologise. I appreciate your patience when adjusting in your mind for this as you read and as you practice.

Chapter Two

IMPACT

FACTS **every golfer must know**

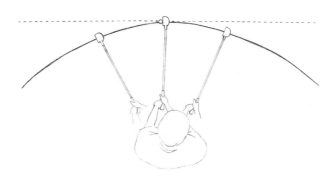

Photo 1

The sweet spot marked on an iron.

Photo 2

The sweet spot marked on a driver.

Finding the club's sweet spot

If you bounce a golf ball on a clubface, you will notice the lines near the centre of the face always deliver the sweetest contact with the ball compared to the rest of the clubface. This is the sweet spot of the club. To be more precise the sweet spot with most clubs is usually found around the 4th or 5th line up from the bottom of the clubface. With the driver, it is normally found just a little higher up the face.

(see Photos 1 and 2)

Photo 3
Pitching Wedge

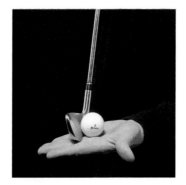

Photo 4
4 Iron

Photo 5
Driver

Photo 6
Pitching Wedge

Photo 7
4 Iron

Photo 8
Driver

Note the shaft angles necessary to find the sweet spots.

SKILL Number 1
Very good ball strikers consistently hit the SWEET SPOT with ALL their clubs.

Good ball strikers use this sweet area of the clubface for virtually all their shots, meaning they obtain a solid consistency to their ball striking. How do they do this?

If you place a lofted club, say a pitching wedge, in the palm of your hand with a golf ball next to the clubface, notice that the only way to get the sweet spot to contact the ball is if you lean the club shaft forward, thus reducing the loft of the club. If we do the same exercise with a longer club, say a 4 iron, we still have to lean the shaft forward to get the same result, but not as much. With a driver, you don't have to lean the shaft forward at all for the ball to touch the sweet spot, if it is teed up.
(see Photos 3,4,5)

If you study the photos of our very good ball striker with the same three clubs, you'll notice the exact same state of affairs with the club shaft positions exist at impact. He has *found* the sweet spot on all three shots.
(see Photos 6,7,8)

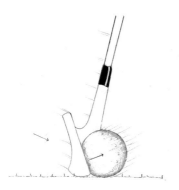

Illustration A

A. Good 7 iron impact, note the contact is nearer the ball's equator, hence more pressure to the core.

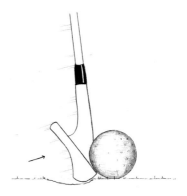

Illustration B

B. Poor 7 iron impact, note the contact is further down away from the equator, hence less pressure to the ball's core.

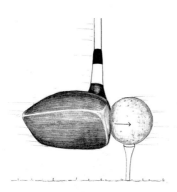

Illustration C - *Driver*

Illustrations C and D.

Note in both cases the shaft does not have to lean forward to pressure the ball's equator.

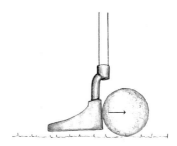

Illustration D - *Putter*

Pressuring the core of the ball

To move a golf ball *forward* powerfully, we have to apply *pressure* into the core of the ball with the club's sweet spot. Because golf clubs have loft (to get the ball into the air), this pressure can only be effectively achieved with the club shaft leant forward at impact, thus striking the ball higher up nearer its equator.

(see *Illustration A*)

If the shaft leans back *at all*, then less pressure is exerted to the middle of the ball and there is a huge power loss. This is because the club's sweet spot cannot connect so easily with the ball. Hence the ball will be struck lower down further away from its equator, because the loft of the club has been increased.

(see *Illustrations B*)

Only with very straight faced clubs ie. the driver and the putter, can we exert pressure into the middle of the ball without having to lean the shaft forward.

(see *Illustrations C and D*)

Attack down

The *only* way to achieve this very powerful "leant" forward effect with the shaft at impact, is to make a *downward* attack to the ball with the *intent* of applying *pressure* into the *core* of the ball!

(see *Illustration E*)

The loft of the club alone forces the ball to rise into the air, the golfer should play no part *whatsoever* in that department and this is *crucial*.

Another major reason why *all* good ball strikers use a descending attack to their shots is because they can accelerate a club head travelling downhill a lot faster onto the ball, compared to a club head which is travelling more horizontally. As the clubs become longer then more speed is developed when the club heads sweet spot collides with the golf ball. Great contact is then inevitable for these players and they *compress* the golf ball onto the clubface.

(see *Illustration E*)

Illustration E

Shaft "lean" occurs naturally with an intentional downward attack to the core of the ball.

Photo 9   **Photo 10**

Photos 9 and 10.

Note the downwardness of the iron attack compared to the shallower less downward attack with the driver.

Illustration F

A descending attack imparts greater back spin to the ball.

If we now study **photos 9 and 10** of our same good ball striker just before impact, notice the very marked *downward* attack of the club towards the ball with the iron, whilst the more straight faced driver is approaching the ball less downhill. The different ball positions make life easier for him to find the sweet spots of each club and to apply the *optimum* pressure to the balls core to produce the best possible ball flight.

Backspin

When the ball is compressed onto the clubface with a descending attack, *backspin* is then imparted onto the ball. Without going into too much detail here, backspin is essential to keep a golf ball in the air longer. It also makes the ball stop quicker when it hits the ground, thus giving the golfer greater *control*.

(see Illustration F)

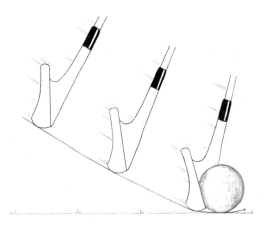

Illustration G

Illustrations G and H.

Hitting off hard fairways and rough is so much easier with a downward attack.

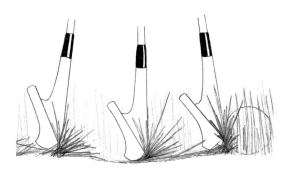

Illustration H

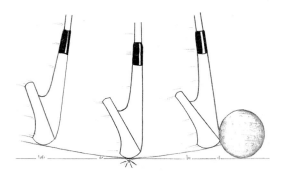

Illustration I

Illustrations I and J.

Note how hard these situations become without a downward attack.

Illustration J

The benefits of a downward attack

The benefits these good ball strikers get from making a *downward* attack at the ball are many and cannot be ignored. Hitting shots from everywhere on the course becomes easier once this skill is acquired. This is why good ball strikers can hit good shots off tight lies when fairways are hard and also they can hit quality shots from the rough too.

(see Illustrations G, H, I, J)

Another *huge* benefit of this skill is that short shots (i.e. pitches and chips) become so much easier; and I will talk more about that later in this book.

However, making a downward attack on its own is not enough to guarantee these good ball strikers a powerful, effortless golf shot in the right direction, time after time. To do that they have to perform two further tasks through impact. These two tasks become more important as the clubs get longer and more straight faced.

Photo 11
Short Iron

Photo 12
Mid Iron

Photo 13
Driver

Photos 11, 12, 13.
To achieve square contact we have to endeavour to strike the ball at the outermost point of the curving club heads path.
This is why, with all good ball strikers, we will always see the club head to the left of the ball prior to impact, when viewing the
shot from "down the line", as these pictures show.

Key
For "down the line" photos the broken
white line represents the target line.

SKILL Number 2
Very good ball strikers consistently make SQUARE CONTACT with the ball.

If the good ball striker is to hit the ball in the correct, intended direction, they are required to hit the ball *squarely* at impact.

Let's study the photos of our good ball striker in the down the line viewpoint taken fractionally before impact.
(see Photos 11,12,13)

Notice how, with all three different clubs being hit, the club head is very clearly to the *left* of the golf ball and not in line with it. It is a *myth* to believe the club should approach in a straight line to the back of the ball, in line with the intended target. Good ball strikers *never* do this, unless they are trying to hit a deliberate slice. What you will find, if you study this pre impact area, is that *all* good ball strikers attack the ball with the club head following a natural curving path from inside the target line *(see illustration N on page 62 for an explanation of "target line")*. They strike the ball at the outermost point of the curve that they are creating in front of them.

Delivering the club head in this way provides the *squarest* possible impact to the golf ball. A square contact will always bring greater accuracy to the resultant ball flight than a non-square contact.

So now, picture a good ball striker using the downward effect mentioned earlier and combining it with a curving inside attack to the ball. They now have a speeding club head approaching impact in the squarest possible way, where they will find a collision with the ball and the sweet spot of the clubface. I think you'll agree, this is a very *powerful* set of circumstances they have created.

But wait, there is one more effect these good ball strikers deliver that creates *even more* power to the resultant shot.

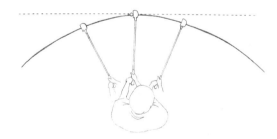

Illustration from above the ball showing how square contact is created.

Photo 14

Photo 15

Photos 14 and 15.
Note the clubface is open before impact and closing after impact.

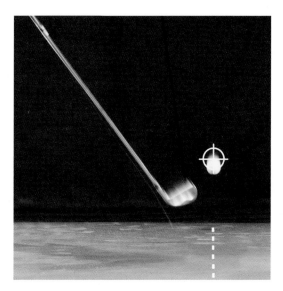

Photo 16 - *Driver*

Photo 17 - *Mid iron*

Photos 16 and 17.
Note the clubhead moving off to the left of the target line after impact in both these photos.

SKILL Number 3
Very good ball strikers consistently create EFFORTLESS POWER.

Study our player again, this time from the face on viewpoints.
(see Photos 14 and 15)

Notice how the club face is *open* before impact and *closed* just past impact. Basically our player has turned the clubface over through impact, just like a tennis or squash player does with a racquet when hitting a ball solidly and powerfully. **(see Illustration K, below)**.

All good ball strikers employ this closing effect with the clubface in golf, but they *always* precede it by making sure they attack with the *inside* curve in the first place. This closing effect naturally continues the curving nature of the attack after impact too, which is why you never see good ball strikers following the target line with their club heads after impact. The club head *always* moves back inside to the left again almost immediately after impact
(see Photos 16 and 17)

Combining the 3 skills

So now we have a club head speeding downhill and approaching impact in the squarest possible way. The sweet spot finds the ball and the club face itself is *whipped* onto the ball with a very powerful closing effect.

It should be of no surprise to you now to understand how these good ball strikers hit the ball such prodigious distances, with such unerring accuracy and seemingly without effort. It should not be a mystery to you now at all. As long as you understand these skills of impact, you can work to apply them to *your* shots. As you practice these skills your ball striking will become better and better. Remember, golf is most definitely *not* a *mysterious* game, it is utterly logical and natural so long as the *task* is clearly outlined to you.

Illustration K
The clubface working from open to closed through impact.

Photo: 18

Clapping in a straight line (from above) VERY unnatural.

Photo: 19

Clapping using a curving attack, very naturally correct.

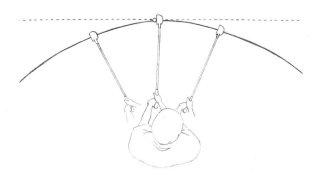

Illustration: L

A very good ball striker uses a similarly natural correct curving attack with a golf club.

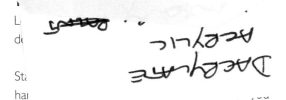

L
de

St;
ha
to ... left hand stationary, and then move
your right hand away to a position approximately
2-3 feet from your left hand but still at waist
height. Clap your right hand back hard to your left
hand but do it with a *straight line attack*.
(see Photo 18)

Do the same thing but this time use a *curving*
attack from *inside* with your right hand.
(see Photo 19)

The latter clap should feel much more solid on
contact (and hurt a little more!) because this is
the best natural way to do it. You will feel the
palms connect *flush* together with this attack,
whilst the former clap might not feel quite such a
flush contact. Doing it the correct,
natural way, gives the feeling of *square* contact.

Now take this exercise one step further. Set
your right hand 2-3 feet or so away from your
stationary left hand and again clap hard from
inside, but this time as you approach impact allow
your right hand to *whip* from open to closed
(like a racquet shot).
(see Photo 20)

I guarantee this will hurt so much, you will not be
able to keep your left hand stationary as the
hands hit – OUCH!! My secondary school
discipline master was particularly fond of this
exercise, as I found out far too often!

Seriously though, if you imagine the right hand is
the club head and the left hand the ball, this
exercise is a brilliant representation of how good
ball strikers apply their club heads to the golf ball.
(see Illustration L).

They add to this only one other thing. That is,
they combine this very natural action with the
downward effect mentioned earlier in this
chapter, so that the club's sweet spot finds the
ball in the process.

Photo: 20
*Adding an opening/closing right hand gives the clap
tremendous extra power.*

Photo 21
Seemingly ridiculous, terribly unnatural clapping action.

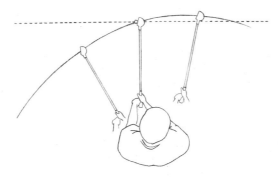

Illustration M
How the majority of the world's golfers apply their club to the ball through impact. (Note the similarity to the above terrible clapping action!)

This downward effect can be felt very easily in the hand clap exercise as well. Simply set up for the clap as before, but this time tip over from your hips until your hands point somewhere down at the ground, reflecting a golf address position. Clap in exactly the same way as earlier. Because you've aimed your arms more to the ground, there is now a natural *downward* move of your right hand to your left as you execute the clap.

Also, notice as you tip over, the more you point your arms towards the floor, the *more* downward the attack with the right hand feels. This represents beautifully the greater downward attack you should use for short irons. If you only tip forward a little and point your arms less towards the ground, then the right hand attack feels less downhill. This represents using a longer club such as a wood. You still have to attack downhill, but less so than with a shorter club.

Do the same with the club head to the ball

When you do the same things to the ball with *your* club head, you will know instantly from the powerful, square contact you get, that you have *achieved your task* and the ball will catapult away effortlessly towards the target. You *really* will feel like you are *hitting through the ball*, just like the right hand whipped itself *through* the left hand in the clapping exercise.

Now when you look back at **photos 11, 12 and 13** on page 28, you now know why you see all the club heads to the inside of the ball before impact, never in line with it, or worse still… to the *outside* of the ball! Remember in the clap hands exercise, the least effective clap was with a *straight* line attack. Do that exercise again now (if your hands can bear it!) and clap the right hand back from *outside.* **(see Photo 21)** The contact this time will feel terrible and very off centred and *very unnatural.*

Unbelievably, this is how the majority of golfers worldwide apply their club heads to the golf ball! **(see Illustration M)**.

Makes you think doesn't it!

The 3 Skills

Skill One

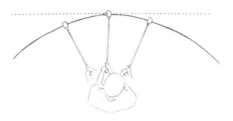

Skill Two

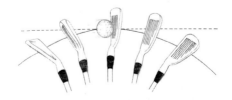

Skill Three

SUMMARY

The 3 skills that ALL consistently good ball strikers use for great impact.

SKILL Number 1

They all attack *downhill* towards the golf ball, at the best angle for each club.

Why? Because it creates acceleration and enables the striker to find the sweet spot of the club and apply more pressure to the ball.

SKILL Number 2

They are all using a *curving attack* with the clubhead and strike the ball at the outermost point of that curve.

Why? Because it naturally enables the striker to deliver a *square* contact to the ball, giving great accuracy and authority to the ball flight.

SKILL Number 3

They all work the clubface from *open* to *closed* through impact.

Why? Because this adds huge power *effortlessly* to the shot.

These are the 3 FUNDAMENTAL SKILLS of golf ball striking that every player *has* to learn if they want to become "consistently good ball strikers." In a nutshell, you have to hit down to the ball in a curve from inside the target line, and turn the blade over through impact. There is no other way to do it.

In the following chapters I will firstly outline to you the correct set of beliefs which will allow the 3 skills to develop naturally. Then I will show you how to practice these skills as you hit balls, until they become ingrained *actions*.

The Promise

As we do this, I promise not to burden you with *any* swing theory at all, but you must promise *me* the same and let go of any preconceived beliefs or theories you may have about your swing or how your body moves. The tasks I will ask you to carry out are best achieved with no other thoughts except *pure* focus on the club, the ball and the intended ball flight
– NOTHING else.

Chapter Three

OUR BELIEFS

**And why nearly all golfers make
the same mistakes**

Photo 22
Fault No.1 *clubhead too low to the ground (scooping), just prior to impact. (Face on viewpoint)*

Photo 23
Fault No.2 *clubhead is to the right of the ball prior to impact. (Down the line viewpoint)*

Having taught the game as intensively as I have for many years now, you might assume that I have seen all manner of swings, and that nothing now is a surprise to me. You would be right. I have witnessed an enormous variety of golf swings, from simple movements to ones of huge complexity, from golfers of all levels of ability.

The TWO faults

The interesting thing is although there is this incredible variety of swing motion in these players, the fact remains that around 90% of them do EXACTLY the *same* things wrong! What are these faults?

No.1. The clubhead is too low just before impact when hitting iron shots from the ground.

No.2. The clubhead is to the right of the ball just before impact with all clubs, *(from a "down the line" viewpoint)*
(see Photos 22 and 23)

That's all. Just two faults!

The chances are very high *(up to 90%)* that you, the reader, will be suffering from either one or both of these problems to some degree, whether you know it or not.

Consistently good ball strikers on the other hand, do not suffer from these faults and that is why they *are* "consistently good ball strikers".

If you correct these errors on a permanent basis, you too will improve your ball striking and consistency beyond recognition. The question is how do we make these changes permanent?

Photo 24

*If the ball is struck at the outermost point of the curving
club head's path, the headcover should never be contacted
before impact. 9 out of 10 golfers usually hit the
headcover when first trying this!*

Key

*For "down the line" photos the broken
white line represents the target line.*

Video can help

Firstly, it is imperative the golfer is made aware of these faults. I tend to use video to do this and film my pupils hitting balls. I then show them their impact zone in still frames from the "face on" and "down the line" viewpoints. They can then see for themselves in crystal clear images, the evidence of the club head's relationship to the ball just before impact. I then compare their impact stills on a split screen next to a very good ball striker. The differences are plain to see. It is a very powerful, awakening image for the pupil to observe. Some are shocked by the differences.

At this juncture, I must stress that at no point will I EVER enter into any conjecture with the pupil regarding the *look* of their swing in comparison with the better player. This, I have found, is where teaching with video can be detrimental to a lot of pupils if they are allowed to dwell on differing swing characteristics. I will *only* use video to highlight their delivery of the club to the ball at impact, nothing more.

Video is not essential though

Now obviously a lot of players will not have access to this type of video analysis, but that doesn't matter. We can still be made aware of the two faults very easily. Here's how.

Firstly, through the *feel* of the clubs contact on the ball. If you hit the ground before the ball a lot, or suffer topped or thinned shots, or get a vibration or dead feeling through the club shaft or you are losing distance because your iron shots fly too high, then I guarantee you will have the club head too low to the ground prior to impact *(mistake no. 1)*. If you consistently get a crisp, sweet contact with the ball and normally strike the ground *after* the ball with your irons, then you do not suffer from this mistake.

Secondly, if you leave a soft object *(such as a headcover)* in the area designated by **Photo 24** and in the process of hitting shots *(use one of your longer clubs to do this)*, you find that the object is being clipped by the club head itself, then you are suffering from *mistake no. 2*.

Now that you are aware of these faults, the vital next step is to understand why you've developed these errors, and why the vast majority of golfers have all developed the same problems.

WRONG BELIEF
Number 1

Photo 25

*The resultant poor impact from the wrong belief that we
have to "get under" the ball.*
Note the shaft leaning back

REPLACEMENT BELIEF

Photo 26

*The resultant good impact when the correct
"attack down" belief is applied.*
Note the shaft leans forward naturally.

Golfers' Beliefs

The reason for these faults lies in the players' belief system and their incorrect perception of how a club head should strike a golf ball. If the player is to *permanently* change these faults, then he first must *permanently* change his belief system *(as to how good shots are struck)*. When the golfer is armed with that superior knowledge, his perceptions of what the club has to do at impact will change and he will be able to meet the task of hitting golf shots crisply, solidly and effortlessly with a supreme amount of confidence.

So what is this "wrong belief system" that lets all these players down and what do we change it to?

The three most damaging beliefs

In my opinion, golfers have numerous misconceptions that hold them back, some more damaging than others. Here I am going to deal with *three* of *the* most damaging beliefs. These beliefs leave the player bereft of any chance to permanently improve their ball striking and lead directly to the two faults mentioned earlier becoming very nasty habits! For each wrong belief outlined here, I am going to give you a *replacement* way of thinking. This substitution *has* to be made *permanent* by *you*. If it isn't then we cannot progress further, of that I am 100% certain.

WRONG BELIEF Number 1

In order to make the ball rise or to make good contact with the ball and avoid topping, the player has to get *under* the ball.

REPLACEMENT BELIEF

In order to find the clubs sweet spot the player must hit *down* towards the golf ball. Good contact and getting the ball airborne are inevitable from this action.

The oh so damaging phrase "get under the ball"

The "get under the ball" mindset holds more players back from improving than anything else. It is *the worst* thing a golfer can think. It leads the player directly away from any possible contact with the sweet spot and makes compression of the golf ball impossible to achieve. When a golfer tries to go under the ball the club shaft always leans back away from the target, **(see Photo 25)** forcing the club head to be *too low* to the ground prior to impact. Even the worlds' greatest players cannot find the sweet spot when this happens.

When the correct "hit down" mindset prevails, the golfer now is naturally encouraged to lean the shaft towards the target at impact **(see Photo 26)**. Compression of the ball and contact with the sweet spot are now highly likely. With the club shaft in this position, the club head is naturally higher off the ground prior to impact, making shots from any type of lie so much easier from anywhere on the course.

For the purposes of your improvement as a golfer, I want you to *abandon* the words "get under the ball" from your psyche FOREVER!
Don't even say it. If you do, give yourself a slap! It's that important!

WRONG BELIEF
Number 2

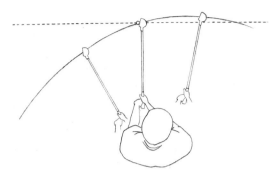

Illustration M

What invariably happens at impact when a golfer tries to swing in a "straight line" through the ball.

REPLACEMENT BELIEFS

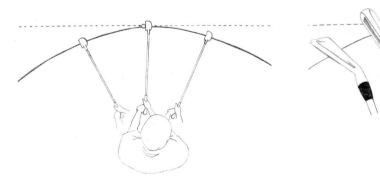

Illustration L

Illustration K

Illustration L and K. Let the clubhead follow a natural curve and allow the clubface to work from open to closed through impact.

WRONG BELIEF Number 2

In order to hit straight shots, the player has to make the club head follow a *straight* line through the ball towards the target for as long as possible, and the clubface itself should remain pointed toward the target for as long as possible. **(see Illustration M)**.

REPLACEMENT BELIEF

There are no straight lines for the club head through impact, except maybe for a very short putt. For every other shot the club head should follow a *curve* and strike the ball at the outermost point of that curve to achieve a square contact. The club face should be allowed to work from open to closed at the outermost point of the curve. **(see Illustration L and K)**.

In other words, just remember the hand clapping exercise we did in chapter two. It mirrors this correct belief utterly and feels totally natural too. Remember, a well-struck straight shot is a result of a *square* contact and *not* from trying to move the club head in a straight line.

Photo 27

Photo 28

In an effort to get the club into a "straight line" through impact, golfers invariably and inadvertently throw the clubhead on an "outside" path prior to impact. As these down the line photos show.

The incorrect and damaging "straight line" mindset

The "straight line" mindset contributes more than anything else to the fact that roughly 80% of all golfers suffer from slicing and pulling in varying degrees and never ever seem able to cure it. As long as the golfer has this belief system in their mind and has probably practiced it hard too, they have no chance of improving their ball striking or curing a slice.

Straight shots in golf have nothing to do with straight lines. Unfortunately, nearly every golfer who tries to swing in a straight line to the ball ends up with the club head to the right of the ball **(see Photos 27 and 28)** prior to impact. If the golfer then tries to work the clubface from open to closed they can pull the ball severely to the left, so this very natural closing action of the clubface no longer becomes an option, so the player doesn't do it. As a result the player is robbed of any ability to achieve effortless power *(skill 3 Chapter Two)* as the clubface cannot really be allowed to close. As the clubface is not closing, slice spin is imparted to the ball. This spin is heightened when the club is more straight faced, which is why so many golfers *cannot* use a driver – the most straight faced club we have, apart from the putter.

All these problems are caused by the *"straight line"* effect. That's where it all starts, from a complete misconception of what causes a straight shot.

Then there are those players who believe the clubface must stay pointed at the target for as long as possible after impact. Even if these players do get the club in the right area before impact, they will still leave the ball out to the right of the target, and will suffer from never being able to generate any real power either. Again a circumstance brought about purely by a misconception of the cause of a straight shot.

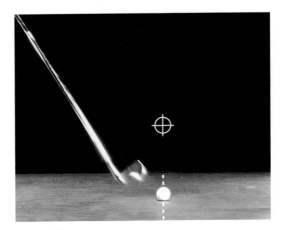

Photo 29

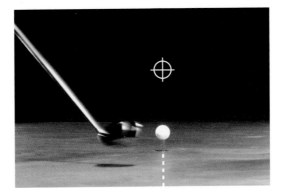

Photo 30

The player who understands that straight shots are a result of "square contact" will deliver the club through impact as the above photos outline. Consequently they will strike the ball at the outermost point of the curving clubheads path.

Square contact creates accuracy

If, however, we think of *square* contact being the cause of a straight shot *(i.e. the hand clap exercise)*, no way would we ever try to deliver the club head to the ball in a straight line. Moreover if we wanted to feel effortless power with the shot and really feel the club head hitting *through* the ball, no way would we ever try to hold the clubface pointing towards the target through impact either. These things would then be the most unnatural hitting actions imaginable.

The point is though, the hand clap exercise is never shown to golfers, neither is how a square contact creates a straight shot explained, so it is perfectly natural for them to assume straight lines equal straight shots. What a *massive* misconception that is!

Now though, you know better than to think like that. I have given you all the information you need to think in the right way, which will lead you inevitably towards straight, powerful shots.
(see Photos 29 and 30)

Never again allow yourself to think in straight lines through impact. Chuck it in the same dustbin as "getting under the ball" – forever!

WRONG BELIEF Number 3

The golfer must keep his head down until well past impact, as this will ensure a good solid contact, and will eradicate topped or thinned shots.

REPLACEMENT BELIEF

Watch the ball 100% of the time, and that means after you have hit it too!

Not only will this short, logical piece of advice save you a fortune in golf balls because you will see where you have hit them. It may also save you from causing yourself physical injury! The reason why is because the much used command "keep your head down", if adhered to, will severely restrict the golfer's natural physical movement and create an inordinate amount of tension in the neck and shoulder region, leading to stresses and strains.

However, the main problem, with this very common misconception, is that it makes performing the correct skills at impact so much harder to do.

The only thing it achieves for some people is that it makes the first two mistaken beliefs easier to perform! Maybe that's why this misconception has such an army of ardent followers. If you want to "get under the ball", and if you want to move the club head through the ball in an extra long "straight line", then yes I would suggest keep your head down as long as possible! Great advice!

However, if you want to hit consistent, crisp, powerful shots, then my advice to you would be to ditch this wrong belief into the same imaginary dustbin as the other two totally wrong beliefs. Don't get we wrong, I'm not saying you should lift your head early, I'm saying pay no attention to your head whatsoever, just keep looking at the ball all the time, the most *natural* thing in the world to do really, when you think about it. Freeing yourself of this tension filled belief will make progress so much easier, and is less strain on your body too.

Remember this, if you top a golf shot it is caused by the fact that the front edge of the club head struck the ball above its equator and nothing else. This can be done with your head held firmly down or with it rising or anywhere else you may want to place it at impact. The fact is, it is of no *relevance* at all. All that *is* relevant is that you keep applying the 3 skills until you get so good at them, that topping a golf shot becomes virtually out of the question.

Don't despair, you're not alone!

Reading through this chapter you may have noticed one, two or all three of these mistaken beliefs are principles in which you believed. If so, don't despair because you're not alone by any means. In fact you have been thinking in the same way as the majority of golfers. To be blunt, the more of these beliefs you held to be true, the poorer the ball striker you probably are.

That may sound brutal, but take heart, because you now know precisely the 3 skills you have to achieve, skills that will improve your ball striking forever. You now have the correct beliefs to help you too. Remember though the good beliefs I have outlined to you are *not* swing thoughts, they are just *understandings* which make the 3 skills a lot easier to apply.

Now I will show you how to practice so that you can put these 3 skills into *action* yourself.

Part Two **practice section.**

"Teaching should be such that what is
offered is perceived as a valuable gift and
not as a hard duty"
(Albert Einstein)

Chapter
Four

HOW TO PRACTICE THE "3 SKILLS".

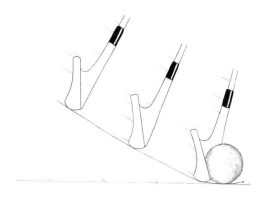

The 3 Skills

Skill One (SK1)

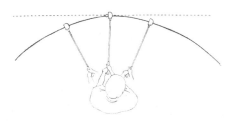

Skill Two (SK2)

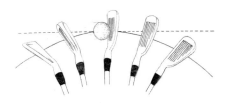

Skill Three (SK3)

By now you should hopefully be quite familiar with "the 3 skills", so from this point onwards I will refer to them individually in the following shorthand:-

SK1
Skill no. 1 – hitting down to find the sweet spot.

SK2
Skill no. 2 – connecting with the ball at the outermost point of the curve for square contact.

SK3
Skill no. 3 – turning the blade from open to closed for great power.

These skills are numbered in this specific manner for very good reasons and it is vital that you stick to this running order when you first practice them. As you progress and become more proficient at them, you will start to notice you can change the balance of the skills in their relationship to each other, to achieve different shots with different clubs. In other words, your natural creativity will come to the fore, which is a wonderful thing. This very normal human exploration should never be suppressed.

It is essential however, that we first learn to walk before we can run, so our primary task is to really practice the 3 skills – individually at first, as their learning underpins all of our creativity that develops later. After practicing them, I will show you how to blend the 3 skills together seamlessly, so they all occur without thought, and your mind is then left free to focus on the golf ball's journey towards its intended destination.

Photo 31

*Place a small leaf or similar loose object just after the tee.
Try to "THWACK" the tee and remove the leaf.*

Photo 32

Now do the same to the ball and remove the leaf

SKILL No. 1

Learning to find the club's sweet spot

To practice SK1 (hitting downhill to the golf ball to find the sweet spot), I want you to hit shots with shorter irons only, wedges through to 7 iron. Do not practice this skill with any clubs longer than this. Probably the best club to start with is a 9 iron. Your immediate *task* with this club is to find the sweet spot when hitting balls *from the ground*. At this point, do not concern yourself at all with where the ball flies, just *try* to find the sweet spot.

Remember, the only way to achieve this task, because of the club's loft, is to hit *downhill* to the ball. Initially, with my pupils, I get them to practice this without hitting balls, but by hitting small tees instead.

Hit tees correctly first

The rubber tees at driving ranges are excellent for this, and give you great feedback to let you know if you are achieving the task correctly. Use a small rubber tee approximately 2 cm high and place a small leaf or similar loose object just after it on the mat **(see Photo 31)**. Your mission now is to hit down with the club with the sole intention of applying pressure to the tee, knocking the leaf away in the process. When you get it right you will hear and feel a very satisfying "THWACK!" as the tee is struck and the leaf will be removed.

If you don't feel or hear this "thwack" sound, you are not hammering the clubhead *down* enough, and not pressuring the tee enough. Just "clipping" the top of the tee or feeling the mat being struck before the tee are also telltale signs of an incorrect attack on the tee. Keep practicing this until you can do it correctly on a frequent basis. One thing I can guarantee you is that if this task is not achieved properly with a tee, it will *not* be any better with a ball!

If you can only do this exercise on grass, then put tees down with loose objects placed just after in the exact same way. When you get the correct contact the tee will most likely fly out of the ground and you'll take a divot where the loose object had been placed.

Then do the same to the ball!

Remember, it does not matter how you swing the club or what length or speed your swing is, or even how you hold or stand with the club. All that matters is that you achieve the task clearly outlined. When you can do it with tees on a fairly regular basis, place a ball on the ground (*not on a tee*) and do the same thing to the ball. Hit downhill to it and try to remove the leaf.

(see Photo 32)

Photo 33

Photo 34

You will most likely find the task (SK1) easier to achieve with the ball placement in Photo 33 as opposed to the placement in Photo 34.

The correct contact is unmistakable

When you get it right, you'll know instantly. The sweet spot will find the ball and you will feel a satisfying contact with no vibration through the club shaft. The ball will ping away up into the air, not necessarily straight yet, but it will *feel great* to hit the ball like that. As your confidence and understanding grows, you will naturally apply more speed to the hit. This is absolutely the right thing to do, so continue with it. If, at some point you seem to lose the good connection, then revert back to slower speeds or even return to the tee and leaf practice, but just get back to achieving the task again, until your confidence grows once more.

Incidentally, as you practice this skill using slower speeds, you will inadvertently be practicing your short game. This is because the major skill that underpins virtually the entire short game *(except putting)* is the knack of hitting down with the club head to make the ball go up. We will come back to the short game later on.

Common difficulties golfers experience with this task

In order to achieve the task outlined, you may notice the job is made either easier or harder, simply by where you place the ball in relation to your body. Experiment with this, but I pretty well guarantee you will find it easier to get the job done with the ball placed opposite the middle of your body, than with it placed more forward of that point **(see Photos 33 and 34)**. This point will seem much clearer to you when you read the next chapters.

Another common occurrence is that players end up *steering* the club down to the ball in an effort to get the task *just right*, or they consciously try to *lean* the shaft forward to find the sweet spot. Both occurrences are *fatal*, and should be avoided at all costs. Instead, freely throw the clubhead as if hammering an imaginary nail into the ball itself. Again this point will become clearer in the following chapters.

Persevere!

Practicing like this is a brilliantly simple way of learning to find the sweet spot with golf shots from the ground, and it really gets you *feeling* the downward acceleration of the golf club to the ball.

If you have difficulty with this task, I urge you to just *keep going* at it, persevere. As long as you hold onto the right beliefs and practice it in the correct way, steering clear of any interfering swing thoughts, you *will* get there. Also take heart, most golfers usually find this the hardest of the 3 skills to perfect. The next two are definitely easier.

Photo 35

(Down the line) shows where the headcover SHOULD be placed.

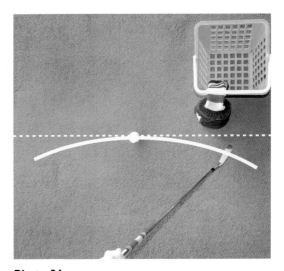

Photo 36

(From above) shows how a correct curving attack will never strike the headcover

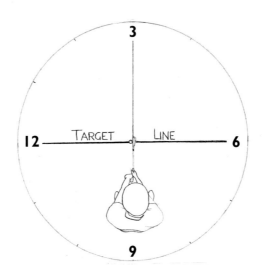

Illustration: N

The imaginary giant clockface laid out on the ground, the golfer hits balls from the centre. He faces 3 o'clock with his body and aims the clubface at 12 o'clock. The "target line" runs from 6 o'clock through to 12 o'clock.

SKILL No.2

Learning how to make square contact

Once you are happy that you can find the sweet spot fairly regularly with your short iron practice, move on straightaway to practicing SK2 *(delivering a square contact to the ball)*. You can use any club you like to practice this, but I recommend you try it first with a five or six iron, then progress right through to the driver as your confidence grows.

Earlier in chapter three we placed a head cover on the ground next to the ball **(see Photo 35)**. If the head cover was clipped by the club head, it told us the club head was outside of the target line just prior to impact. Not a good situation. So our task now, if we leave the head cover in the same place, is to make a square contact that will avoid hitting the head cover altogether. **(see Photo 36)**.

Clap your hands

Before hitting any shots though, I want you to do the hand clap exercise again a few times, to reinforce to yourself why we are practicing this skill. Picture your right hand is the club head and your left hand is the golf ball as you perform this. It's *very* important that you do this first.

Imagine a giant clockface

Now I need you to use your imagination. Picture that you are hitting balls standing directly in the middle of a *giant* clockface that is laid flat on the ground. As you stand in your address position to hit balls, you will be facing directly opposite 3 o'clock *(assuming you're a right hander)*, and if you hit a dead straight shot from there, it would fly directly at 12 o'clock. So an excellent way to describe the "target line" is that it is the line that runs from 6 o'clock right through the middle of the clock face to 12 o'clock **(see Illustration N)**.

Hitting balls now, I want you to face 3 o'clock in your address position and then aim your clubface at 12 o'clock. However, as you attack the ball at impact, try instead to hit the ball straight out towards 1 o'clock on the clockface. Keep doing this until you get the majority of your shots starting out *right* of the target line. If you can also apply SK1 as you do this, even better. Just remember to move the ball position a little further forward as the clubs get longer and more straight faced, so that you will find the sweet spot.

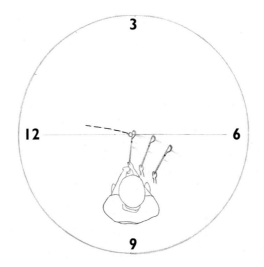

Illustration: O

A curving attack from inside the target line will produce shots that start out to the right of 12 o'clock.

If you are achieving the outlined task, the head cover on the ground will *never* get struck by your club head during impact and virtually *all* of your shots will start out to the *right* of the target line, not along it. **(see Illustration O)**. If this is the case, CONGRATULATIONS, you now have the club in the same delivery position prior to impact as *all* good ball strikers! This is all that's required at the moment. Don't worry where the ball finishes up. This is immaterial.

At this point in proceedings I can fully understand you saying,

"why then, do good ball strikers not hit the ball straight out to the right all the time?"
The answer very simply is that they apply SK3, which is to turn the clubface from open to closed during impact. When you have the club in the above correct delivery position, SK3 is actually a pretty straightforward skill to apply, even at very high speed.

A common scenario with less skilled ball strikers is that they try to apply SK3 without really having any idea about SK2 and its vital importance. Their club heads tend to approach impact too much along the target line, or worse still from outside it, and as they apply SK3 the result can be some quite horrendous shots to the left. SK3 then pretty well gets abandoned, - (due to the high price of golf balls), and is replaced instead with a weak steering action through impact. The ball doesn't go as far, but it's much less expensive!

This is why it's so important to practice and apply these 3 skills in the correct order, and not to get *ahead* of yourself. The fabulous SK3, which delivers amazingly effortless power, simply *cannot* and *must not* be applied until skills 1 and 2 have been practiced first.

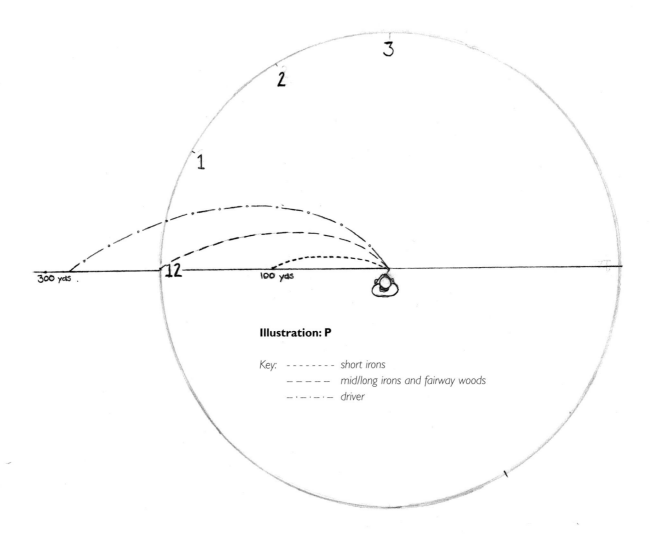

Illustration: P

Key: - - - - - - - *short irons*

 - - - - - *mid/long irons and fairway woods*

 -·-·-·- *driver*

SKILL No.3
Learning how to achieve effortless power

To practice SK3, I want you to use your imagination again. Stand to the ball exactly the same as before, facing 3 o'clock with your body and aiming the clubface at 12 o'clock. Now I want you to *picture* the ball flying straight out to 1 o'clock again, but this time imagine it curving right to left in flight (*draw shape*) back towards 12 o'clock **(see Illustration P)**.

(Notes for Illustration P).
The times on the clock face are merely MENTAL images the golfer should picture when initially practicing and learning the 3 skills. They are NOT intended ball flights. The purpose of this imagery is to enable the golfer to EXPERIENCE the feelings of where good ball strikers have the club just prior to impact, until they get used to it. If a player doesn't experiment with this imagery, it is highly unlikely he will ever get the club into the correct pre-impact positions.

It is also a good idea to adjust the mental image when practicing with different clubs.
For example:
Short irons *– picture the ball starting out right between 12 and 1 o'clock*
Mid to long irons and fairway woods *– picture it starting out to 1 o'clock*
Driver *– picture it starting out between 1 and 2 o'clock.*

With all the clubs though, picture the ball returning back towards 12 o'clock, our intended destination for the shot.

Think draw

Focus purely on the club head and the ball and the intended big *drawshape* ball flight you see in your mind. This *imagery* is enough to get SK3 happening. The clubface will work from open to closed through impact, in a similar way that a racquet hits a ball forward with immense power in tennis or squash.

When you get it right you will be amazed by the results. The ball will probably not start out as far right as you imagined. It may just fly dead straight or it may start a little right of 12 o'clock and draw back. Either way it will feel *fantastic*. It is a real jaw dropping moment for many golfers who have never experienced a *true* draw like this before. For me it is one of the best moments in teaching when this happens, just to see the expression on the pupils face. Money cannot buy the feeling I get from helping someone to achieve this and I never grow tired of it.

Feel skills 2 and 3 with baseball swings.

If you hold a club up in front of you at roughly waist height, and then proceed to make practice swings on a horizontal level, similar to a baseball player, you will start to feel skills 2 and 3 happening quite naturally. Notice how easily the club swings in front of you in a natural curve, *never* a straight line. Also, you will sense the clubhead turning from open to closed very naturally at the outermost point of the curve. You may also notice that this action occurs more easily with a light grip pressure as opposed to a tighter one. I will expand upon this point later.

The logo for 3skillsgolf™
represents the balance of the 3 skills.

Practice, practice practice!

Remember, you only have to hit one shot like this to prove to yourself you CAN DO IT. After that it's your job to practice to make sure you get this wonderful feeling as often as possible, and believe me you will *want* to practice it!

The more you practice these glorious skills, the more permanent they will become. At first it may feel strange to intend to hit the ball out to the right so much, especially if you've been an habitual slicer, but get yourself used to the feeling because it is *utterly* correct. The hand clap exercise will help enormously to make sense of it all. Keep referring back to it to reinforce the very natural feeling it promotes. Very quickly it will seem just as natural to apply the club head to the ball in the same way as the hand clap, and it will seem wholly *unnatural* to think in any way that straight lines equal straight golf shots!

See it and do it!

After some practice, you will be able to hit wonderful golf shots *without* thinking about clock faces or turning the clubface over at impact. This is the point where applying the 3 skills has started to become an ingrained *action*. This is a great situation to be in, it frees the golfers mind to focus more on ball flight and the outcome of the shot envisaged. Put simplistically SEE IT AND DO IT!

The balance of the 3 skills

The result of every single golf shot we hit, from any point on the course, comes from a balance between the 3 skills and our application of them at impact. The job for each of us is to work out *our easiest* way to deliver these skills on a *consistent* basis, at club head speeds with which we are comfortable. It is not our job to think about *swing*. The swing itself is only a *vehicle* to deliver the 3 skills. That vehicle can have hundreds of different variations as to how it operates. Luckily the 3 skills have only a small number of variations, but those variations take care of virtually every shot you ever need to know.

When practising the 3 skills it is quite normal that you may over or under emphasise each skill when experimenting with the balance. As a result, you will hit poor shots as well as some very good ones. Experiment with it though as much as you want. This is how you will *learn*. It is so important you *feel and understand* a whole range of shots made possible by the mix of the 3 skills.

The 3 Skills

Skill One (SK1)

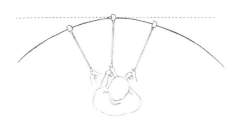

Skill Two (SK2)

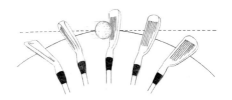

Skill Three (SK3)

Practice wisely

If you consistently see a certain type of poor shot happening when you practice, change your emphasis on the skills. Try not to keep repeating a mistake. Remember, the answer *always* lies in the balance of the skills. Also bear in mind the order of practice I gave you in the previous chapter. Working on SK3 with a driver at the start of a practice session, before you've considered SK1 and SK2, would not be the wisest approach for example.

A better way would be to start by practicing SK1 with small wedge shots, progressing to more powerful shots with your short irons, introducing SK2 and SK3 along the way. Then progress to your mid and longer clubs. If you struggle at all, just go back to smaller shots again with SK1 in mind. Treat this as your foundation work in *embedding* the 3 skills. It is essential practice work to build a lifetime of good ball striking.

As your confidence grows and your practice improves, experiment with different ball flights on your shots. Visualise it first, then try to produce the shot within the parameters of the 3 skills. Never *pollute* this approach with outside swing theory. All that will do is cloud your focus on the visual image you have built in your mind.

So whether your shot is good, bad or indifferent, you *never* need to look outside of these skills for an understanding, an improvement or a variation of that shot.

The more correct your beliefs and understandings of impact are, the easier it is to deliver the club to the ball time after time in the way you want.

The more you practice, the more skilled you will become in your application of the tool, the golf club, to the ball. You will be able to craft shots, as shot makers do, making the game so much *more fun* to play. You will visualise shots on the course that seemed impossible to you before.

You may notice also that your best shots on the course may happen when you are faced with the trickiest circumstances. Eg. Hitting out low from under trees and running the ball between some bunkers onto a green. In these sorts of situations you are *forced* to *focus* on an outcome that has only one available option, so you *visualise* the shot so much better.

However, only with practice and an understanding of the 3 skills in the first place would a shot like that ever be possible for you.

Chapter Five

FORGET SWING!

Instead . . .
"make the task easier for yourself"

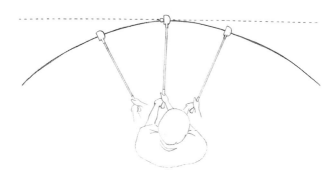

Here is a list of 10 truly great golfers past and present, with some observations often made about them by golf teachers and writers:

Jack Nicklaus: *the greatest ever, huge powerful hip turn, left heel lifted high off the ground at the top.*

Ernie Els: *modern day great, very little hip turn, left heel firmly on the ground at the top.*

-- • --

Nancy Lopez: *legend of the game, extremely slow tempo with very strong right hand grip.*

Ben Hogan: *legend of the game, lightning fast tempo with very weak right hand grip.*

-- • --

Lee Trevino: *multiple major winner, consistent tough competitor, open stance, swings outside going back reroutes the club inside coming down.*

Ray Floyd: *multiple major winner, consistent tough competitor, very flat and inside going back reroutes the club back squarely coming down.*

-- • --

Jim Furyk: *major winner, supremely accurate, rarely misses a fairway, highly unusual looping swing, very outside going back.*

John Daly: *major winner, probably the straightest ever long hitter, highly unusual long swing, very inside going back.*

-- • --

Bernhard Langer: *major winner, flat back swing, very strong left hand grip, great iron player.*

Jose Maria Olazabal: *major winner, very fast tempo, very weak left hand grip, great iron player.*

These ten golfers listed opposite are some of the finest exponents of the game ever. They have performed *consistently* well at the highest level of their sport for virtually their entire careers. These player's golf swings have stood the test of time, under the greatest of pressure.

Studying their swings more closely however, reveals differences in style that are quite enormous. They *all* have highly individual motions that are *all* highly effective. Long held "bad swing traits" that teachers have frowned upon for many years, are seemingly used with wild abandon by these players.

If we were to create a list of "generally accepted" fundamentals required for "good golf", along the lines of correct grip, posture, alignment, takeaway, swing plane, tempo, halfway back and top of the back swing positions, then according to these principles, these ten players would not stand a chance of playing "good golf".

The TRUE fundamentals of golf

If though we take the "*true*" fundamentals of golf, the 3 skills, as being the key to "good golf", these 10 players now become perfect role models. All of them execute the 3 skills perfectly at impact time after time, as do *all* top ball strikers.

The message should now be clear, NOTHING is as important in golf as the TRUE FUNDAMENTALS.

The golf swing develops and evolves *naturally* around your application of these three principles. The *worst* thing you can do is to think about complex elements of your swing in the *hope* your ball striking will improve. The *best* thing you can do is forget about your swing and instead practice the 3 skills as outlined until they become ingrained actions. As you do this try to make the task of applying the 3 skills *easier* for yourself. Let me explain further.

Photo 37

With the club lifted up in front of you to waist high, check to see if the leading edge is vertical.

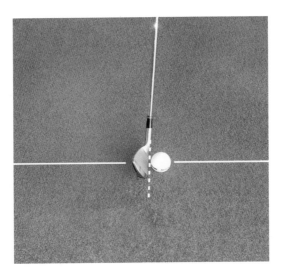

Photo 38

Keep it this way as you lower it down next to the ball. (Note the leading edge is now at right angles to the target line).

Club face position at address

If we think again about hammering a nail into a block of wood, I think it would be fair to say that everyone would start by hovering the centre of the hammerhead squarely over the top of the nail. The anticipation of driving the nail home would naturally bring about this circumstance prior to the hammer being drawn away. This is not a rule, but it may make the task *easier* to perform.

When we place the club head next to the golf ball in the address position, it is a similar situation, I think you'll agree. I also think it is sensible to aim the club face in the same direction as the intended target, in the anticipation that the club face will arrive back squarely at impact in a similar position as address. This all seems obvious really.

However, I have seen so many golfers *not* do this at address it is uncanny. Also, virtually all of these golfers have no idea that their club faces are not aiming anywhere near their intended target. Not a particularly good starting point.

If you want to start with the club face pointing in the direction of your target, and again it's your choice, a good way to make it easier is to lift the club head up off the ground vertically in front of you and then check to see if the leading edge *(groove line no.1)* is vertical. If it isn't you are probably not aligning the club face squarely to the ball at address.

Try to make sure the leading edge is vertical in front of you, and then lower it down next to the ball. As you lower the club down next to the ball remember the clock face. If you are facing 3 o'clock, as long as you keep the leading edge vertical on the way down, then the club face *has* to be pointing towards 12 o'clock when it sits next to the ball.

(see Photos 37 and 38)

It also makes a lot of sense to position the club head's sweet spot directly opposite the back of the ball, while in the address position.

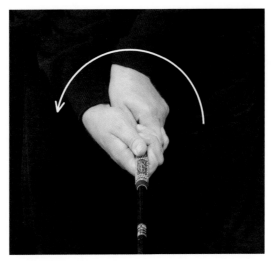

Photo 39
Both hands twisted to the right.

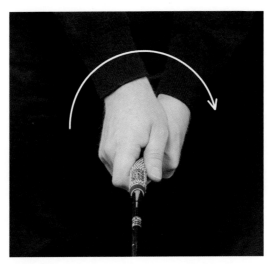

Photo 40
Both hands twisted to the left.

Grip

I place no rules upon my pupils as to how they hold the club, it's their choice. However, I do show them the different influences exerted on the club as a result of changing their hand positions and grip pressure. Then I let them experiment and decide for themselves how they want to hold the club for the best result. Let me give you some examples:

Grab a golf club and hold it up at waist height in front of you. Keeping the leading edge of the club face vertical, twist both of your hands right over to the right on the grip so that your right palm faces more up and your left palm more down. **(see Photo 39)** Notice how difficult it is now to open the club face, but how dead easy it is to close it.

Do the opposite now. Twist both hands to the left of the grip the same amount. **(see Photo 40)** Notice how easy it is to open the blade but very difficult to close it.

Also notice that the more the club sits in your fingers as opposed to your palms, the easier it becomes to rotate the club face from fully open to fully closed.

When we now consider SK3 and what we have to do with the club face at impact, you may want to experiment with different grips until you achieve a good comfortable balance. Don't be frightened to explore this – it's how we learn.

Again I place no rules upon my pupils. If they change their grip it will be their choice, so they gain a better, *easier* execution of the 3 skills and, as a result, a much improved ball flight. They will have a much greater understanding of *why* they are doing it, rather than just being *told* how to grip the club.

On the whole, players having difficulty closing the club face through impact and suffering weak shots leaking to the right, may want to explore gripping towards photo 39 in varying degrees.

Conversely those players who find they can close the club face too easily and normally get good contact but suffer from too many shots hooking low and to the left, may want to explore gripping more towards photo 40 in varying degrees.

The 3 Skills

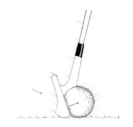

Skill One (SK1)

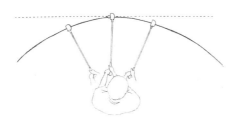

Skill Two (SK2)

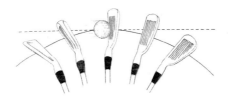

Skill Three (SK3)

Grip Pressure

Players that understand the 3 skills, and especially SK3, will evolve a grip that supports these skills rather than a grip which hinders them. These players also will evolve the correct grip pressure, which again makes it a lot easier to execute SK3.

I have found that poor ball strikers, unaware of the 3 skills, are nearly all very wary of the club face opening and closing too much at impact. They think it leads to all of their errant shots. Because of this belief *(usually married to a belief in straight lines)* they try to eliminate any "flippiness" with the club head at impact by gripping the club very *tightly*. If SK1 and SK2 aren't being applied either, then gripping the club tightly might be a good thing to do initially. However, this situation will *never* lead to any significant long term improvement for a golfer. If anything, over time they will get worse and more frustrated with the lack of any real power in their shots.

In my estimation, based on years of teaching experience, a majority of golfers grip the club too tightly. However just telling them to "loosen up the grip pressure a bit", is of no help to them whatsoever. If they want to achieve real, effortless power with their shots, they have to understand why they are lightening the grip pressure, and why SK3 is so important.

This is why I believe the correct grip pressure for each player will evolve over time as they are practicing and exploring the 3 skills. Remember, everyone is different. Even the very best players will have variances in their grip pressure, but they will have discovered through practice which pressure is best for them.

A final word on this subject. Sometimes hitting shots from poor lies, such as heavy rough, may require an increase in grip pressure to avoid an early twisting of the club face at impact. Doing this will nearly always lead to a power loss. This is quite normal and should be taken into account when executing the shot.

Photo 41

Short iron. Note the ball position in the centre of the stance.

Photo 42

Mid/long iron. Note the ball position is more forward.

Photo 43

Driver. Note the ball position is at its furthest forward.

Ball position

The following examples of ball position can also make it easier to apply the 3 skills.

If you know the shaft has to lean forward at impact to find the sweet spot of a very lofted club, then the centre of the stance will probably be a good option.

If you place the ball too far back to achieve this, you may well drive the club too heavily into the ground and de-loft the club so much, that the ball will fly out very, very low. This can actually be a very skilful, *deliberate* shot to use when playing against very strong headwinds, or when trying to escape low from overhanging trees. Without experimenting and exploring though, you would probably never learn about this shot.

Conversely, playing the ball too far forward may make it very difficult for you to find the sweet spot. You may lose your balance trying to execute the shot properly.

If you are using a more straight faced club, you may notice better results in ball flight with the ball placed a little forward in the stance, simply because these clubs require less shaft "forward lean" to find the sweet spot. Ultimately a driver doesn't require any real shaft "forward lean" at impact, so keeping the ball well forward may give you the best results. Again, explore and experiment.

(see Photos 41, 42 & 43)

A simple appreciation here of hammering nails through the ball at the three different angles, as outlined in chapter six, will make these changes in ball position seem very natural and logical.

Just choose a position to stand to the ball that makes hammering the nail at the right angle easier for you.

(see chapter six regarding this)

The 3 Skills

Skill One (SK1)

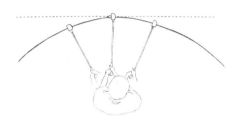

Skill Two (SK2)

Skill Three (SK3)

Posture

Similarly, you should experiment with the distance from the ball as you use different clubs. Standing closer to the ball and leaning over more may make it easier to hit short irons where SK1 is important, but you may need more space to hit longer clubs when SK2 becomes more relevant, so standing further away and leaning over less may make this easier for you .Therefore your posture at address will *evolve* with practice to support your best application of the 3 skills with differing clubs.

You will find the greater your confidence becomes in delivering the 3 skills at speed, the more athletic your posture will turn out to be. This is a natural evolvement based on the anticipation of delivering controlled *speed* to the ball at impact.

Baseball is a great example of this. If you ever get a chance, try this out. Lob balls gently to the batter, ask them to just tap the first ball gently forward a few yards, but then tell them to hit the second ball as hard as possible. Watch how immediately *athletic* their posture becomes for the harder hit with no prompting at all.

The same way, we see a different posture in a good golfer for a little chip shot as opposed to a long drive. It should be a natural change brought about by the anticipation of different force being applied to the hit. This leaves the golfer comfortable at address rather than stiff or tense due to the *rules* of posture.

THE MYTH OF THE FULL SWING

When the 3 skills are explored for smaller shots such as pitching, you can really get some great results very quickly – feeling effortless power and great control with it. To add more distance to your shots, gradually increase the speed that you deliver the club head to the ball, but try to retain your feeling of control as you do so. Do the same with your longer clubs too.

With the application of greater speed, it is inevitable your back swing and follow through will become longer. This will happen naturally. To the onlooker it will appear that you are now making a normal full swing and hitting the ball crisply, with great control and distance.

Problems only arise when the golfer believes that this is somehow not good enough, and what they are doing does not feel like a *full swing*.

This is because they are programmed to believe a full swing includes a minimum 90° shoulder turn and 45° hip turn for the back swing and a set of similar *rules* for the through swing. They also believe that the club itself must move into certain positions throughout the swing.

When golfers try to apply these standards to their swing, their minds are diverted from the simplicity of the 3 skills, and instead focused on swing technique. Unfortunately, it's all too much thinking, and focus on the real task is lost.

Don't think about your swing!

My advice is this. If you want to make it easier to apply the 3 skills, *don't* think about swing theory *at all*. When you look at tour pros or any good ball strikers, they all execute the turn and the follow through in a different manner anyway. Some turn their shoulders more than others, some turn their hips very little while others turn them a lot. Some players move to the right when turning back, some do not. Some keep their knees apart while others do not. Some players have very long swings while some are much shorter etc., etc., etc. The through swing and follow through will have similar variations.

The question is which one is right? In my mind they all are right as long as the 3 skills are delivered consistently well. Golf swings are only wrong when the 3 skills are not applied correctly.

So which one of these thousands of different swing variations do you choose for yourself? It should be comforting to know a good swing will happen to you anyway as long as you apply the 3 skills at a speed with which you are comfortable. The length and shape of that swing is totally immaterial. You will have a swing which is *effective*, the only swing worth having.

So what exactly is a full swing?

It is the limit at which each individual golfer can deliver their maximum speed to the hit whilst retaining good control of the 3 skills. This limit will be different for every player, and can only be determined by practice and experimentation.

There is no industry standard full swing, neither are there any swing rules to which you should abide.

Therefore every golfer can develop their *own* full swing and their *own* set of rules to get the job done. This is what the ten great golfers mentioned at the start of this chapter have done so brilliantly throughout their careers.

Remember, as long as the 3 skills are applied correctly, *any* swing, however it looks, is correct!

HOW SPEED IS MISUNDERSTOOD

A lot of golfers are frightened of applying speed to their swings. Many believe they have to swing slowly to produce the right rhythm or tempo, and that this will somehow give them the precision timing they need to hit good golf shots.

Unfortunately, this is a recipe for a player to get worse rather than get better.

When they swing the club slowly, they believe they can assimilate all the swing thoughts and positions they have been given to think about, so they can get everything *just right*. Any application of speed will then ruin their plan for the swing, so they believe swinging too fast is the root of all their problems and they *sloooow* it all down!

The trouble is they have then robbed themselves of the natural dynamics which need to be there to apply the 3 skills effectively and consistently.

Tempo and Rhythm

Now don't get me wrong, I'm not telling you that you've got to swing quickly, I'm saying don't think about it at all, neither quick or slow. Just swing at a speed from which you know you can comfortably deliver the 3 skills consistently well.

Maybe through practice and the better your 3 skills become, your confidence in swinging harder and faster will grow, enabling you to hit the ball great distances and with total *control*. It's really down to each individual golfers own talent as to how far they can take this. This is what separates *great* ball strikers from just *good* ones. It is a natural evolution within the sport itself.

My advice is to again set your own rules in this department. Do not be bound by other peoples' rules. When you look at tour players, they all show wide variations in the speed of their swings going back and through. Some take more time to get the club back to the ball than others, but when you measure their club head speeds at impact they are all very similar give or take a few *m.p.h.* More importantly they are all comfortable with their own swing speeds and they deliver the 3 skills consistently well.

Eventually you will settle upon your OWN even tempo or "rhythm" that you can apply to all you shots. This will make it easier for you to be CONSISTENT with your ball striking, and it will give you good DISTANCE CONTROL, a common trait among all good golfers.

Photo 44

Seven iron showing an even wear mark.

EQUIPMENT -

The right lie angle for you

The choice of equipment available to golfers these days is vast and ever changing. Only by experimenting and trying out different clubs and shaft flexes will a golfer be able to decide if one club is better for them than another.

Remember this though. Buying expensive golf equipment is not guaranteed to deliver any significant improvements in your ball striking. *Only* an improvement in the 3 skills can do that.

However, having said that, there is one area of your golf equipment that is *hugely* important you have correct – the *lie angle* of your irons.

Even if you have applied the 3 skills perfectly and achieved a square contact at impact, if the lie angle of the club head to the shaft is not correct for *you*, hitting a straight shot is *not possible*.

You can easily test this by attaching some white masking tape to the base of your irons and then hitting some shots from a mat. If the wear mark on the tape is even **(see photo 44)**, that is the correct lie angle for *you*. If the wear mark is not even, if it is either just at the toe end or the heel end of the club, then the lie angle is incorrect for you and your clubs must be altered or replaced. See a good quality PGA club fitter if this is the case. IT IS ESSENTIAL.

Remember, testing the lie angle can only be achieved by hitting shots. The lie angle of the club in your *address* position means nothing at all and should be disregarded.

Part Three

playing on the course section.

*"The less you think about your swing,
the better you will play"*

Chapter Six

NAIL IT

Making it work for YOU on the course

Now that you have practiced the 3 skills individually, it is essential that you are able to blend these skills together seamlessly until they occur virtually with no thought at all.

The reason for this is straightforward. If we are to play our best golf on the course, we cannot afford to fill our minds with too many thoughts other than where we want the ball to go and how it should get there.

The hammering philosophy

In chapter one I referred to how we think when we hammer nails into a block of wood. As this task is so clear we pay very little attention to technique, and instead focus very clearly on driving the nails home with a good, solid impact. If we happened to mishit some of the nails, we would not require coaching to help us but merely time to practice hammering more nails in a better way!

Imagine if we could transfer this simple, highly logical philosophy to hitting golf balls. After all, golf clubs are really just lightweight hammers of varying lengths with angled hitting faces. They are designed for the purpose of applying pressure to stationary golf balls to make them move in certain ways. In the same way hammers pressure stationary nails and force them to move.

Not a great deal of difference really! Why then is the game portrayed in such a hugely complex manner and why can't we we think of it this simplistically when we hit golf balls?

My answer to that is YOU CAN!

IF YOU KNOW HOW THE TOOLS WORK!

Unfortunately, if no one tells you how the clubs should work it is impossible to employ a philosophy as simple as hammering nails. Instead, you have to focus on the complexities and idiosyncrasies of the human body and all its movements. Tricky stuff to say the least!

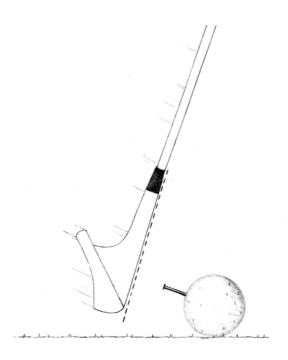

Illustration Q

Shows a short iron attacking an imaginary nail set at 20°,
the dotted line represents the imagined hitting face.
Note how the shaft leans forward naturally. (de-lofting)

Nail it with the 3 skills instead!

The 3 skills outline to you exactly how to operate the tool of the golf club, so you get the best out of it by literally hammering pressure into the core of the ball. If you visualise driving nails into the golf ball with the correct clubs for the job, this will put you in control and make the ball fly brilliantly. As long as you can picture the nail being driven into the ball at the correct angle, and you can visualise the ball's flight to its target, the club will do the job it is designed to do. Allow me to elaborate.

Illustrations Q, R and S show an imagined scenario of three different types of golf clubs hitting nails into balls at three differing angles. (Note - in all scenarios the imagined nail is always parallel with the target line).

The short irons

Illustration Q shows an ideal attack scenario for a short iron. You should imagine driving a nail downwards into the ball at an angle of roughly 20 degrees. If you can picture that the clubface is hammer like and without loft, *(similar to a hockey stick or a putter)*, and that it is this imaginary clubface which hammers the nail, then you will achieve the best contact with the club and the ball. The ball will catapult away from the sweet spot with power and backspin.

If the task is perceived and executed in this way, note how the handle end of the shaft will always end up ahead of the ball at impact *(sometimes referred to in golfing terminology as de-lofting the club)*. This situation you will *always* see at impact when good ball strikers hit their short irons. This has always been seen by golf teachers as notoriously difficult for average golfers to achieve. However if you successfully hammer a nail downwardly at around 20 degrees, then you could not do anything else but de-loft the club. More importantly you would have achieved this without thought, simplifying matters enormously and keeping the mind *clear* to focus more on the intended ball flight.

Note also, because of the nail's angle how the club would inevitably strike the ground *after* the golf ball *(just as all good ball strikers do)*. This explains why good ball strikers always take their deepest divots with short irons.

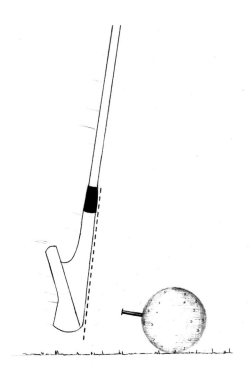

Illustration R

A mid/long iron attacking an imaginary nail set at 10°.

The mid to long irons

Illustration R shows an ideal attack scenario for a mid to long iron. You should now imagine a nail being driven into the ball in the same way as before, but at a shallower angle, this time approximately 10 degrees. Again picture the clubface as flat without loft and you will get the best contact.

Executing the task in this way again naturally de-lofts the club a little at impact, but less so than for the short irons. Also, it will encourage a slight divot to be taken after the ball but less deep than with the short irons.

You may also want to experiment hitting your more lofted woods, rescue and hybrid clubs at this angle too.

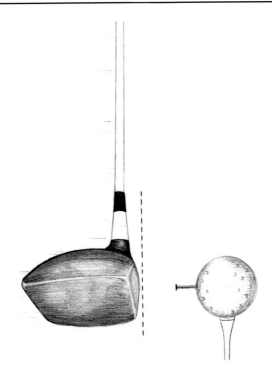

Illustration S

The driver attacking an imaginary horizontal nail.

The driver and 3 wood

Illustration S shows the ideal attack scenario for a driver. You should imagine a nail being driven into the ball horizontally.

This naturally produces a brilliant result as the near vertical face of the driver pummels the equator of the ball forcing maximum pressure into the core of the ball. Now the handle end of the club stays more or less level with the ball at impact and no divot will be taken at all. The ball is launched into the air due to the club's 10 degrees or so of loft.

When using the 3 wood I would encourage you to think of hammering the nail horizontally too, However, tee the ball down much lower to the ground than the driver for the best results.

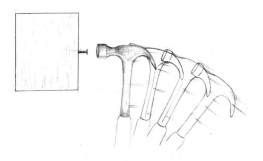

Illustration T

Shows good natural hammering.

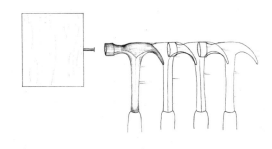

Illustration U

Shows poor, unnatural straight line hammering.

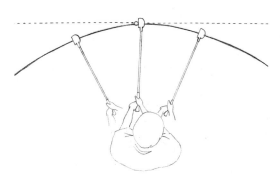

Illustration L

Reflects good, natural hammering.

Make square contact

If you look at **Illustration T** it depicts (*from above*) the action of someone hammering a nail into a post. Try to picture performing this task yourself. Notice the natural curving attack path which creates a solid square contact with the nail. Trying to execute this task in a straight line **(see Illustration U)** would be absurd, and a solid, square contact nigh on unachievable.

This scenario is exactly what golfers are faced with every time they use their drivers. The driver itself is essentially a straight faced hammer designed to strike the equator of a golf ball squarely, the same way the hammer drives the nail into the post. This is why you never see very good ball strikers delivering the clubhead to the ball in a straight line. It just doesn't make any sense to do it that way!
(see Illustration L)

Superb ball striking will occur though if you *combine* attacking the imaginary nail at the correct angle for the club being used, and strike it in the *squarest* possible way. This is depicted by the very logical, natural way we would hammer nails into a post. (*The hand clap exercise in chapter two is another brilliant, natural representation of this concept.*)

Photo 45
Practice striking the tee with the basket handle placed as shown in the photo.

**A practice tip to get the best
out of your driver!**

*Only practice this with your driver,
NEVER any other club!*

When you practice at a driving range, I want to
show you a brilliantly simple way to get the best
possible contact with your driver.

You should now know and understand we are
endeavouring with a driver to hammer an
imaginary horizontal nail through the centre of
the ball. Hence if we place the handle of the ball
basket as outlined in **photo 45**, and we attack the
ball in the correct manner, we should never
contact the handle or the basket. However before
you go rushing in to try this, I can guarantee up
to 90% of golfers will clip or strike the handle if
they go in straightaway with their usual full
attack. That's why this is a task which needs to be
approached with a little measured caution to
avoid damage to your driver and other
people's property!

I always start my pupils with very small practice
swings, as if just tapping a nail home horizontally. I
get them clipping the tee and we gradually build
the speed as they get more confident. I do not let
them hit balls with the handle in place as this can
be a little distracting. Just take your time practicing
clipping the tee without contacting the handle
and you will gain invaluable experience of how a
really good driver of the ball delivers the club at
impact. They pummel the equator of the ball.

When you feel ready, take the handle away and
hit balls continuing to imagine that the nail is
there to hammer home horizontally, picturing a
powerful drawshape ball flight!

Incidentally, you may have noticed from this book
that all the tools you ever need to become a
great ball striker are freely available to you at your
local golf range, i.e. rubber tees, leaves(with any
luck!), head covers, baskets, golf balls and golf
clubs. This information itself will save you a
fortune in buying expensive teaching aids and
gadgets, which rarely serve any purpose other
than giving the player even more irrelevant things
to think about!

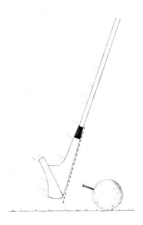

Illustration Q

Shows 20° nail angle for short irons.

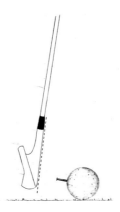

Illustration R

Shows 10° nail angle for mid/long irons and fairway woods.

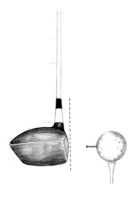

Illustration S

Shows horizontal nail for driver and 3 wood.

Attack the ball with these nail angles in mind and you will have unlocked the secret of striking all your clubs well on the same day.

Striking all the clubs in the bag well on the same day

I think you'll all agree that if the above happens to us then we can guarantee a great day on the golf course. But how often does this situation ever take place?

In my experience, this very rarely happens and usually the higher the players handicap the less chance there will be of it happening. So many times you will hear a golfer complain that "my woods were great today but my irons appalling" or "my short irons were good but my long irons terrible" or "my long game was all right but my short game rubbish" etc., etc. You hear it all the time. Why?

I believe there is no mystery behind this at all, in fact it's quite obvious. Firstly, every player should understand that golf is a very skilful game and hitting all the clubs well is no easy task. However the task is more or less impossible if you have no appreciation of attacking the ball at different angles with different clubs!

If though you appreciate the three different angles of attack outlined with the nail illustrations **Q, R, S**, you will have unlocked the secret of how to strike all your clubs well on the same day. No easy feat for any golfer but at least now you should *understand* what is required to achieve it and you can practice accordingly. Not knowing or choosing to ignore the angle of the nail will make it impossible to achieve any form of consistency in your ball striking, the contact you get with different clubs will be a complete lottery.

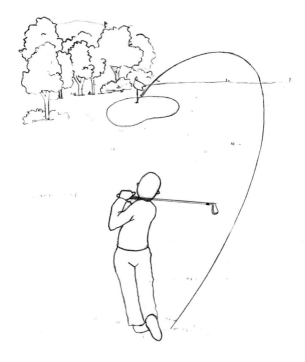

Chapter
Seven

THE CRUCIAL IMPORTANCE
OF IMAGERY

Making it work for YOU on the course

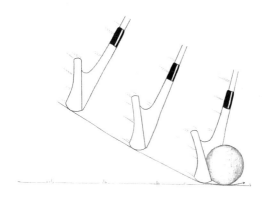

*'Imagination is more
important than knowledge'
(Albert Einstein)*

The left and right brain

Scientific research has shown that the human brain is composed of two hemispheres, the left brain and the right brain. The two hemispheres can work together, or independently, processing information and controlling our actions.

The left brain is commonly referred to as the "analytical brain", and is thought to control logic and reasoning. The right brain is different, and is thought to be responsible for creativity, intuitiveness and, interestingly, athletic ability.

In golf because the ball is stationary, there is a lot of time for left brain activity to occur. This is where analytical, complex swing thoughts can easily take over, and leave no room for right brain creative thoughts. Sports played with a moving ball (tennis, squash, football etc.) are more reactionary, and leave little time for left brain analysis. This is why many people find these sports easier to excel at than golf.

We simply have to accept the nature of golf and the way it is. Therefore to play well, we have to get both halves of the brain working together harmoniously.

Visualisation

Good golfers all have the ability to *visualise* their shots before they execute them. This is good right brain activity, and I believe *essential* if a golfer at any level is to play their best golf.

However, I also believe that the image we picture in our mind has to be reconciled with left brain logic and its understanding of how the club will produce that imagined outcome.

Focusing on the logic and simplicity of hammering the ball solidly and squarely at the right angle, so the club will do its job, will satisfy the analytical mind. The player is then able to form an image with the creative mind of the ball flight and its destination.

This is the ideal situation for a golfer, when the two hemispheres operate together harmoniously and in tandem.

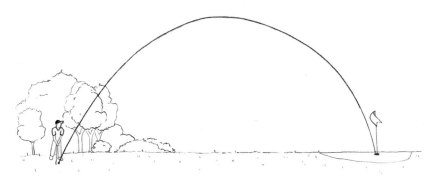

Illustration V

How most golfers "picture" the trajectory of a pitching wedge. Unfortunately this "rainbow like image" is not a good one to have in mind.

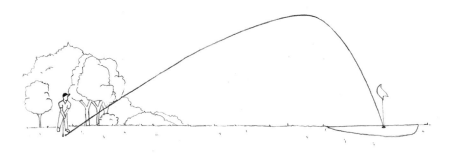

Illustration W

This piercing "bullet like" trajectory is much better for a golfer to picture.

Correct and incorrect imagery

Having asked many of my pupils about how they visualise their shots, I've learned that most golfers have an incorrect picture in their mind of their desired ball flight. This in turn affects their left brain analysis of the shot and brings about confusion as to how they should operate the club through impact.

Unless the golfer has the correct picture of ball flight beforehand, they will not be encouraging themselves to execute the 3 skills of impact successfully. Allow me to explain further.

Picture bullets not rainbows!

If you ask an average golfer to describe the trajectory of say a pitching wedge shot from a side view point **(see *Illustration V*)**, generally they will depict a looping trajectory, like that of a rainbow. Unfortunately this is not a good image to have in mind.

The reason why is because if you accept that it is the loft of the club that gets the ball airborne and that alone, then you should accept that the ball trajectory will always start out at 90° to the clubface at the point of impact **(see *Illustration F* on this page)**.

If then you are perceiving a looping flight this can only be achieved by scooping the ball through impact with the shaft leaning back. *(As we know, a very poor impact situation)*.

Whatever the ball flight pictured, a golfer will use the club accordingly to produce that image.

It makes no sense at all therefore to image a rainbow trajectory. Instead try to picture a *piercing, bullet* like ball flight **(see *Illustration W)*.**

If you see it this way, then you will have effectively *eliminated* tendencies towards the dreaded scoop, and your ball flight will generally be lower and more penetrating. This is ideal for all conditions, but absolutely vital for trickier, windy days when control of ball flight is essential.

I believe it is a good thing to picture all shots having this bullet like trajectory. The difference in each club's loft will produce different heights in the ball flight, and the backspin created by better contact will make the ball grip well on landing. All good ball strikers display these characteristics in their shots.

Illustration F
Shows a golf ball taking off at 90° to the club face

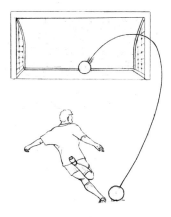

Illustration: X

Shows a footballer "picturing" kicking towards goal.

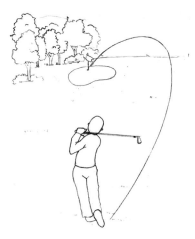

Illustration: Y

Similarly, how a golfer should "picture" hitting a shot to a destination.

Picture draws not straight lines!

When asking pupils to describe the imagined direction of their ball flight to a target from an aerial viewpoint, the usual reply is that they picture the ball flying there in a straight line.

Although in reality this may be a very good outcome, I believe very strongly that this is a poor image for the average golfer to picture prior to hitting a shot.

The reason why is because most golfers, in their attempt to achieve this, will *(a)* try to move the club head through the ball in a straight line and *(b)* keep the club face pointing towards the target for as long as possible. As we now know, good ball strikers never do these two things. Because they are a recipe for a slice!

Remember over 80% of golfers suffer from slicing the ball to varying degrees, and never really cure this fault. I believe this occurs to a majority of them because they *picture* and *try* to hit shots in a dead straight line. Only golfers who picture the right to left *draw* shape ball flight and experiment and practice it, will effectively be curing a tendency to slice.

A brilliant analogy to this is the kicking of a football towards a target. Imagine yourself kicking a football from the centre circle of a football pitch into an empty goal ahead of you. Admittedly this is a very difficult task for anyone, but no way would you ever picture the ball flying towards the goal in a straight line! If you were kicking with your right foot you would always see the ball curving out to the right and returning back towards the goal. **(see Illustration X)** Trying to do this task in a straight line would be extremely difficult even for top footballers.

With golf, when imaging a draw shape starting out to the right of your target and returning to it **(see Illustration Y)**, you will actively be encouraging *(a)* a square contact and *(b)* turning the clubface from open to closed through impact. We now know, all good ball strikers, do both these things.

When trying this, what you may notice happening sometimes is that you actually achieve a *dead straight shot*. But it will have been nothing to do with imaging a dead straight ball flight!

In my opinion all golfers should experiment and practice trying to draw the ball as a means of curing slicing and ultimately, hitting straight shots.

See it and do it!

When golfers learn how to eliminate scooping and slicing from their games, and instead play with penetrating draw shots, the game suddenly becomes *so* much easier and more *fun* for them.

Without correct imagery though it is virtually impossible to change a golfer's bad habits at impact. This is why a lot of golfers never improve their ball striking.

So many times over the years I have heard pupils say, "I'm not interested in doing fancy things like drawing the ball, I just want to hit it straight!" Unfortunately this mindset will never allow the pupil to improve their ball striking or achieve their goal of straight shots.

But if you picture hammering the ball, and image a bullet like, draw shaped ball flight to your target, you will then activate the 3 skills of impact instinctively. Getting the left and right brain working harmoniously really will allow you to "see it and do it!"

Pre shot routine

All serious golfers should develop a "pre shot routine". This is basically a preparation for each shot which should *never* vary.

Not only is this a good way to build consistency, it is also a very useful means of overcoming nervousness on the course, especially 1st tee nerves. If you focus on your routine and rigidly stick to it, it can stop negative thoughts creeping in and help you to control your nerves during that crucial period when you are taking your shot. It does not matter what this routine consists of, just that it works for you and you resist varying it. Again this is not easy and you will have to practice it. Watching tournament players you will see how disciplined they are in this area, but it is something they practice very hard.

I am often asked by pupils "should I take practice swings before hitting my shots on the course?"

Here are my thoughts on that issue:-

Practice swings versus waggles!

I believe the purpose of a practice swing is to make a dress rehearsal for the shot you are about to hit. You may or may not agree.

If you do agree, then let me give you three reasons why I am not a devotee of practice swings being part of the pre shot routine.

1. If you are rehearsing an iron shot from the ground then you would always have to take a divot with your practice swing, and you know how bad that looks!! (If you don't take a divot with your iron practice swing you are effectively rehearsing a thinned or topped shot).

2. You would never make a practice swing to rehearse hammering a nail into something! But you might use a *waggle*!

3. They slow up play.

Don't get me wrong, I'm not at all against making practice swings as a way of limbering up. I'm just not a fan of them as part of a pre-shot routine.

Instead, use a small waggle which actually rehearses hammering a nail into the ball. This really focuses your attention. Much the same way a snooker or pool player draws the cue back and forth rehearsing which part of the cue ball to hit. Also, you could tailor your waggle with different clubs to suit the different nail angles mentioned earlier.

Once more, it will take practice to develop this but it does make an awful lot of sense!

The only time I would advise making practice swings as part of a pre shot routine is for the short game ie. pitching, chipping and putting.

Chapter Eight

THE SHORT GAME

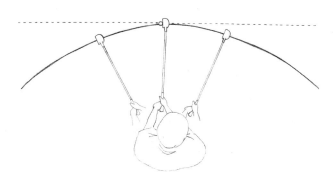

The 3 Skills

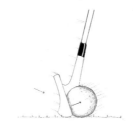

Skill One (SK1)

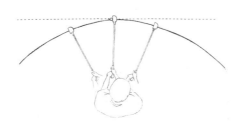

Skill Two (SK2)

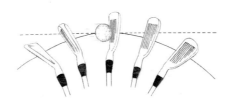

Skill Three (SK3)

WHAT IS THE DIFFERENCE BETWEEN PUTTING, CHIPPING AND PITCHING?

To sum it up briefly:-

PUTTING
– is using a putter and making a square contact, tapping in an imaginary nail that is set horizontally into the equator of the ball.

CHIPPING
– is using a lofted club and making a square contact, tapping in an imaginary nail that is set at a slight downward angle into the ball.

PITCHING
– is using a lofted club and making a square contact, tapping in an imaginary nail that is set at a slight downward angle into the ball, while allowing the clubface to work from open to closed.

Putting

I think we can all agree that putting is the easiest golf shot to learn. Everyone can have fun playing crazy golf at the seaside, we don't need crazy golf coaches to help us! The task is very clear, a flat faced tool called a "putter" hits the equator of the golf ball and it rolls along the floor. Dead simple, that's all there is to it. The only skill required is to hit the ball at the right speed in the right direction. Basically just tap horizontal nails into the balls equator as squarely as possible, the harder you hit them the further the ball will roll.

To become good at putting, it is essential you achieve a *square* contact, this will create accuracy and a reliability in the strike that you will become dependent upon. Remember a square contact can only be brought about in golf by a *curving* attack, and yes, putting is no different. Admittedly very short putts require a relatively straight line attack, but as the putt gets longer, then a curving path for the attack will become necessary for a more authoritative, square contact.

The only time a square contact could be achieved with a pure straight line attack along the target line, would be if the shaft angle were vertical and inserted into the middle of the putter head (croquet style). The rules of golf outlaw this design. So even the games ruling bodies insist you make a curving attack, if you want a square contact.

Consequently the closer you stand to the ball and the more upright the shaft becomes, the less curving the putterheads path should be. The further you stand from the ball and the less upright the shaft becomes, the more curving the path should be, if you want *square contact*.

My advice is, "do whatever is comfortable", but make sure you achieve "consistent square contact" when putting. If you do, then judging the correct distance to hit the ball is a lot easier. Inconsistent non-square hits will make distance control a lottery, ie. more luck than judgement.

Practice hard at your putting, it's unbelievably important if you want to play off a low handicap. Also remember this, most good putters simply have a good imagination and see the putt tracking towards and into the hole before they hit the ball. They "see *it and do it*."

Chipping

Chipping is very similar to putting except the task is to get the ball into the air for the first part of the balls journey towards its destination. This is normally so the golfer can avoid obstacles in the way of the shot. To do this we have to use a lofted tool.

Do pretty much everything the same as putting but imagine you are tapping an imaginary nail downhill into the ball, this enables you to find the clubs sweet spot. When that occurs the ball *has* to get in the air, it has no other choice! Golfers get chipping wrong when they fail to trust this happening and instead opt to try to lift the ball up into the air.

Experimentation and exploration are the key here to you learning a whole range of chip shots of differing heights and lengths. Try chipping with lots of different clubs, you can even try doing it with your woods. Also experiment with the ball placement in relation to your feet. For example, if the ball is placed too far forward in your stance, you may find it difficult to chip the ball from the sweet spot with your wedges, but you may find this not be the case with a more straight faced club.

Explore and experiment but also understand how you can make life easier or harder for yourself with the ball placement. Remember the *only* rules that I will bind you to are that to get a square contact from the sweet spot you have to apply SK1 and SK2.

Pitching

Pitching is without doubt harder than chipping or putting and the reason why is simply because it requires an application of all the 3 skills. Chipping and putting only really requires skills 1 and 2.

Pitching is very similar to chipping but we simply have to add in SK3, (moving the blade from open to closed through impact). This immediately adds in more power to the shot as the ball will *spring* into the air with backspin attached to it. This is incredibly useful when we are faced with a situation that requires a shot with height, distance and grip as it lands.

The distance we hit pitch shots is determined by how much speed we apply at impact. Learning different speeds comes with practice, much like when we learn to hit putts different distances, this can only really be achieved by *feel* through repetition.

Again experiment and explore with different clubs and ball positions but I don't think I need to explain that a more lofted club will create naturally more height and backspin than a straighter faced club. Hence, if you required a pitch and run shot, a club such as a 7 iron may be preferable over a sand wedge and vice versa if you required a high, quick stopping lob shot.

You will notice that by applying SK3, it really gives you great distance to your shots without any feeling of effort and should highlight where *real power* comes from when applied in conjunction with SK1 and SK2. Learning to pitch properly I believe is a brilliant way to practice and really learn about the 3 skills. Every golfer should devote a large amount of their practice time to this shot as they are *embedding* all of the 3 skills by doing so.

Bunker shots

Shots from sand are a logical application of the balance of the 3 skills combined with the effect of sand being involved between the clubface and the golf ball.

For long fairway bunker shots, treat it as if it were just a very tight lie on the fairway and apply all the 3 skills as normal, just make sure you choose a club with enough loft to get over the front lip of the trap.

The sand shot that I'm going to deal with here in a little more detail is the shorter greenside bunker shot. This type of shot is virtually the only time in golf where the clubface should not contact the ball at impact, instead there is a small cushion of sand between the two, which tends to deaden and *soften* the ball flight. Hence this is why we can use a fair amount of club head speed but the ball doesn't travel as far as usual.

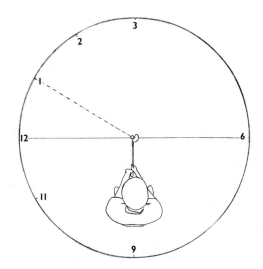

Illustration Z

Note, the golfer faces 3 o'clock, but opens up the clubface to point at 1 o'clock.

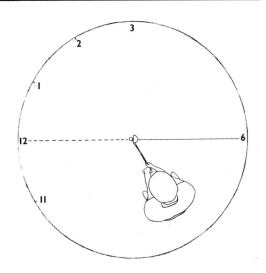

Illustration Z1

Shows how the golfer has "walked around" the clockface till he faces 2 o'clock. The clubface now points at 12 o'clock.

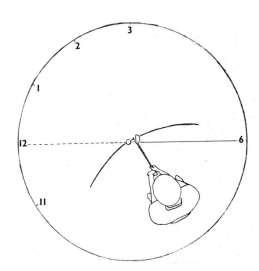

Illustration Z2

When executing the shot picture hitting the nail into the sand before the ball (towards 11 o'clock), NOT along the target line.

The clock face greenside bunker shot

When faced with a standard greenside bunker shot I want you to adopt a central ball position and use the clock face imagery as before.

So if 12 o'clock is your target and you are facing 3 o'clock, firstly rotate the sand wedge in your hands until the clubface points open towards 1 o'clock.

(see Illustration Z)

Now alter the position your body faces – towards 2 o'clock, by *walking* one hour *around* the clockface. **(see Illustration Z1)**

This order of events will have the effect of pointing your clubface *now* in the direction of 12 o'clock. It may feel now as if the ball is further forward in your stance, in reality though it is still in the same central position to your feet, if you have correctly "*walked around*" the clockface.

When you execute the shot hit down towards an imaginary nail that is set in the sand just before the ball, this time imagine the nail is pointing towards 11 o'clock and *not* along the target line. **(see Illustration Z2)**

Try to hit the sand first and try to eliminate any tendency towards SK3. This will have the effect of holding the blade open as it cuts through the sand. The ball will pop up with backspin and travel only a short distance. Practice and repetition of this will give you the feel you need to hit this shot different distances with either more or less club head speed.

Playing shots such as this last one could be perceived as being quite advanced and I would agree. However, to a player with a good grounding in the 3 skills this actually now makes this quite advanced shot actually much easier to understand and to execute. It is just another really good example of how great expertise can evolve with changes in the balance and application of the 3 skills.

Perfect your pitching first, would be my advice, then have fun with highly imaginative, skilful shots like this greenside sand shot.

"We can't solve problems by using the same kind of thinking we used when we created them"
(Albert Einstein)

Conclusion

Chapter Nine

CLOSING THOUGHTS

The problems with conventional teaching

On a golf course there can be many distractions to disrupt our concentration from the job at hand. It has to be accepted that this is just part of the game. But, thinking about the golf swing is a distraction created entirely by ourselves. It doesn't have to be part of the game.

The problem with conventional teaching is that it inevitably gets us thinking about our golf swing. If we accept that nearly all of us play our "best golf" when our minds are free of technical swing thoughts, and we "just see the shot and hit the ball". Why then do golfers feel it necessary to fill their minds with endless, counter productive swing theory! It just doesn't make any sense, if you want to play your "best golf"!

If golfers spend practice time productively and work purely at the 3 skills, then they will have simplified the game enormously. They can then relax in the knowledge that playing golf on a golf course is no more complex than hammering imaginary nails into golf balls at different angles with angled hammers called golf clubs. Their minds will be free to focus clearly on the outcome of the shot and nothing else. This is how we all feel when we play our "best golf"!

Conversely for golfers who have spent their practice time focussing on their golf swing, and its endless technicalities, the last thing they are actually doing is simplifying matters. In reality they are giving themselves too much to think about when they go out to play. If their golf goes awry on the course they then have to think more and more about the elements of their swing to get it "just right". As they are doing that their focus is being increasingly distracted from the real task – the outcome of the shot. Instead they are pre-occupied with the complexities or the "look" of their swing.

The way the game is taught generally and also presented to us by the media, supports and encourages this very fragile state of affairs and does very little to *simplify* it at all for golfers.

"We can't solve problems by using the same kind of thinking we used when we created them" (Albert Einstein)

A very very interesting quote, from one of the most brilliant minds of the 20th century. Let me give you an example of this:

A golfer may come to see me complaining of poor, inconsistent ball striking. In other words this player is not finding the sweet spot or making square contact. Watching this player (a right handed golfer) hit shots, I notice there is a very pronounced sway to the right during the back swing. Finding the sweet spot for many of his clubs is not going to be easy neither is making a square contact. A lot of people might then say that some back swing tuition is required to stop the sway. Finding the sweet spot and making square contact would then become easier at least for certain clubs.

This may well be true, and in the past I would have done this as a teacher, and tried to sort out the player's back swing problem.

Now, I realise that I'm not helping the pupil if I do that!

The reason? Because we should first be asking "why is this golfer swaying so far off to the right in the first place?"

The cause will be because of former back swing tuition, ie. keep your left arm straight, swing back as low and as wide as possible, make sure you shift your weight to your right side, turn your left shoulder over your right leg etc. etc. And on top of this the golfer will probably be thinking "I gotta get under the ball too!".

No wonder a sway develops!

Now, if I tell this golfer not to sway, they will think "well how do I get my weight shifted and my shoulder turned, keep my left arm straight and retain width and NOT move to the right? This game is so FRUSTRATING!!"

I'm sure you will recognise and empathise with this scenario yourself.

The way I coach now focuses the pupil instead on the task of finding the sweet spot of their clubs. I give them logical, simple advice and a task to achieve at impact. Amazingly what I have found is that as the pupil focuses on the impact task their ball striking improves dramatically and their back swing changes inadvertently. What's more, they will have cleared their mind of totally unnecessary swing thoughts, and will no longer complain that "there's just *so much* you have to think about!"

If we look at the conventional teaching approach, where the pupil is encouraged to think about their back swing, there could be some short term improvement. The problem, however, is that the pupil will be misled into believing it was the back swing tuition which led to their progress. The real source of improvement, impact, gets overlooked.

Inevitably, the following happens. The pupil over emphasises the back swing tuition. It may happen after one hour, one day, one week, one month .... but it will happen.

The advice not to sway to the right becomes a lean to the left instead, and now the pupil requires more back swing tuition. This time the advice has to be return to swaying back to the right again but not as much as before!

This scenario will continue endlessly for golfers. There will be no conclusion to it. The worst thing about it all is how it distracts the golfers' attention from the real task, and wastes valuable hours of practice time which could be spent so much more productively.

The answer is to forget about your golf swing. Remember, golf swings happen anyway as a result of applying the 3 skills. Unclutter your mind, spend your practice time productively hitting golf shots, not thinking about golf swings.

All the swing mechanics you ever need eg. wrist set, shoulder turn, leverage, torque, through swing rotation etc. will occur naturally by applying the 3 skills. Believe me, I see it everyday when I'm teaching.

Conventional golf teaching does not simplify the game for golfers at any level, and is becoming increasingly complex in its approach. This in turn is putting more and more people off taking golf lessons. I can fully understand why.

The job of a golf teaching professional is to *help* golfers of all levels improve their golf. It is not to sound off on how much they know about the golf swing. Personally I have learned more from listening to my pupils than anyone else. It made me understand their difficulties with the game. I could then work out the best way to help them. Listening to the alleged top teachers and their complex, conflicting approaches only served to make me more confused and that did not help me get the best from my pupils.

I truly think that golf is a simple sport, albeit a very skilful one. No one can master it totally, that's what makes it so appealing. However, all in all it is basically a game of hammering skills, and if we can teach those skills in the most simple and logical way possible, the better it will be for the majority of golfers.

Keep it a simple game and you will be rewarded for your hard work in practicing it that way.

If you choose to perceive it in a more complex manner, there is no guarantee your efforts will be rewarded. In a lot of cases it leads to the opposite effect. You get worse at the game.

Don't let that happen!

Keep it simple, hammer the nail home and let the club do the work!

"Any intelligent fool can make things bigger and more complex. It takes a touch of genius and a lot of courage to move in the opposite direction." (Albert Einstein)

Testimonials

"Joe's simple yet brilliant technique of concentrating on striking the ball at the correct angle eliminates the need for endless, and usually futile, swing analysis. The confidence which Joe's teaching has given me has enabled me to improve my game and to steadily reduce my handicap."

Joy Starritt - New Malden GC
09/08/2006

"Since having lessons with Joe I have reduced my handicap from 36 to 18. His simple, uncomplicated approach has made a huge difference to my game."

Gill Stedman - St. George's Hill GC
09/07/2006

"I started playing golf on a regular basis back in March 2003 with friends and enjoyed the game tremendously. It wasn't until I attended a corporate golf day and proceeded to hack my way round the course that I felt something wasn't quite right.

After my dismal experience I decided that lessons were in order and booked six lessons with Joe the very next day. In just over two years I have gone from being a non-handicapper to playing off a handicap of 19. The help and advice I receive from Joe is uncomplicated, clear and makes total sense.

Thank you for making a potentially very difficult sport seem easy!!!"

Stephen Leddington - Hersham Village GC
24/07/2006

"I first went to see Joe Hagan as I had completely lost my confidence in my ability to play and enjoy a round of golf. At that time my handicap had frustratingly gone up to 16. Joe's lessons were a revelation, simple and easy to understand. He completely restored my confidence and enjoyment in the game again.

In less than two months I have reduced my handicap down to 12!"

Nuala Lalor - Fulwell GC
21/07/2006

"I first started having lessons with Joe Hagan two years ago when my handicap was 18. Currently, in July 2006, my handicap is down to 10.

I can relate to the way that Joe teaches because he explains things in a simple way that make perfect sense. One of the major things he has taught me is that when I am out on the course, to think only of the two feet before the ball, the way the club head will strike the ball and to picture the flight I want the ball to take. This takes all other swing thoughts out of the equation leaving me free to focus on what really matters."

Shirley Difrawy - Foxhills GC
17/07/2006

"Just wanted to say a big thank you for the improvement in my game since I took lessons with you last year. From not being good enough to even play off a 28 handicap I am now playing off a handicap of 22 and winning matches! By eliminating my slice and consistently hitting straighter shots my whole enthusiasm for the game has gone up unbelievably."

Steve Ellis - Hersham Village GC
21/12/2006

"At the age of 66 through taking lessons with Joe I have dropped my handicap from 24 to 15.6 over a seven month period playing in stableford and medal competitions and have won 9 prizes.

Before this I was stuck on a 24 handicap and not improving at all no matter what I did with my golf swing. Joe's teaching has made me understand how the club does the work and how I don't need to think about my swing at all. My ball striking has improved no end and I am really enjoying my golf again."

Geoff Wright - Hoebridge GC
01/09/2006

"After 35 years as a 15 handicapper, golf seemed to be just plain hard. Taking lessons just gave me more things to worry and get confused about, so I avoided them and experimented with endless personal theories on the range. After a particularly poor patch a friend recommended seeing Joe Hagan for some advice and I booked a series of six lessons. The results were amazing!

Five trophies and a handicap cut to 9 followed within a few months, all beyond my wildest expectations. Sure golf will never be an easy game, but Joe's revolutionary simple approach gives you the best possible chance. He got me thinking about all the other sports that seem to come so naturally which you don't have to analyse in excruciating detail, eg. squash or baseball. A baseball player never agonises over when to bend the left knee or straighten the right wrist, he just swings naturally, just making sure the bat is square at impact.."

"Why can't golf be as simple? Well thanks to Joe, it can be!!"

Tony Harris - Air Products GS
15/07/2006

"The thing I like about Joe Hagan is his communication skills. The elements of the 3 Skills Golf School are articulately put over to make the student feel comfortable in the subject they are learning. My handicap plummeted from 12 to 5 in around 18 months, I don't think this would have been achieved with any other teacher."

Iain Millan, Chobham GC
30/05/2007

"At last ... a golf tuition method that works. In my opinion Joe Hagan has formulated a teaching style that is not only logically sound, but also, clear and concise in a very understandable manner. I cannot speak highly enough about this. There is no doubt in my mind that the 3 skills Joe concentrates upon do work and personally, this has been reflected in my current level of play."

Nigel Chappell - Hersham Village GC
10/12/2006

I started playing golf just over a year ago. On doing so I was advised by a friend to have some lessons from Joe. His simple yet effective teaching methods have assisted me in reducing my handicap from 26 to 16. I would not hesitate in recommending Joe and his team to any level of golfer.

Aidan Baker - Burhill GC
22/07/2007